FEAR NOT!
LEARNING FROM YOUR CANCER

FEAR NOT!

Learning From Your Cancer

JUDY GATTIS SMITH

*A guide for beginning a cancer survivor group
in your local church*

DISCIPLESHIP RESOURCES

PO BOX 340003 • NASHVILLE, TN 37203-0003
www.discipleshipresources.org

ISBN 978-0-88177-538-9

Library of Congress Cataloging-in-Publication Data

Smith, Judy Gattis, 1933-
    Fear not! : learning from your cancer / Judy Gattis Smith.
        p. cm.
    ISBN 978-0-88177-538-9
    1. Consolation--Study and teaching. 2. Cancer--Patients--Religious
life--Study and teaching. 3. Cancer--Religious
aspects--Christianity--Study and teaching. 4. Healing--Religious
aspects--Christianity--Study and teaching. I. Title.
    BV4910.33.S54 2008
    248.8'6196994--dc22
                                        2008023172

This book is dedicated to my beloved sister, Gloria, whose cancer struck swiftly in the midst of her busy life; to my Mother, who suffered so long and intensely with cancer, but never lost her trusting faith; and to my closest childhood friend, Betty Ray, who died of cancer much too young.

Special thanks to . . .

- All the precious, brave, funny survivors who took my survivor classes and added so much to this book. Thank you Jackie Matze, Bob Bensen, Sandy Thompson, Shelva Mounts, Gloria Pearson, Jane Jones, Jo Washburn, Rev. Al Schrader, Jean Venner, Sara Jo Pitts, Elaine Davia, Nan Hodges, Jewell English, and especially Fay Austin who took my class twice. Thank you Pat Broaddus, Barbara Haga, Mary Jordan, Bob Lewis, Larry Thornton, Maureen Sachleben, Nancy Woodlief, and especially Mary Ellen Campbell. Thank you Julie Wilson, Janet Hitch, Sarah Lomax, Betty McCoy, Dana Hanlon, and Cindy Smith. There would be no book without all of you.
- The Hawthorn Center, a unique place in Richmond, Virginia, where cancer patients, families, and friends can gather for social and emotional support, classes and workshops, all free of charge, and special thanks to RobinYoder, the guiding light of the Hawthorn Center.
- Writers of countless books who chronicled their cancer journey, but especially Sharon M. Carr, a person I never met but whose honest, gripping book, *Yet Life was a Triumph*, is the best I have ever read on this experience.
- Bill Zimmerman, also a person I have never met, but whose upbeat books energize me, whose correspondence encouraged me, and whose generosity overwhelms me.
- The many people who worked on the production end of this book but especially my editor, George Donigian, who believed in this project, gave it a name and was responsible for getting it published. Thank you, George.
- My husband of over 50 years, David Smith, who lived the cancer experience with me, holding my hand through the rough days, and who shares our shining, remaining days.

Table of Contents

Preface

Everyone who has been diagnosed with cancer has a personal story to tell. The good news is that the cancer experience is more than a personal story. Being diagnosed with Non-Hodgkin's lymphoma was the beginning for me of an incredible learning experience. I had been very active all my life (name a group and I joined it) but I was always aware that there was something more—a great mystery that I would someday explore. When told that I had cancer, when brought face-to-face with my own mortality, I was surprised at my first reaction. I remember thinking, "What good timing! I have just finished the summer unit in Sunday school that I was teaching."

"Now where did *that* come from?" I later wondered.

"What am I? A Pollyanna?" Where were any profound thoughts about life and death?

This was my first awareness that there was a lot about myself and my faith that I would learn through this cancer experience. Yes, it's painful, embarrassing, humbling, degrading, depressing, disgusting, and frightening. There is no whitewashing it. But there is also so much more to this experience.

As my cancer grew and the intensity of treatments increased, I began to write down what I was going through. There was a lot of reflecting on questions such as, "Why me? Why *not* me? Where am I now? What next?"

When I was able, I began to read what other persons affected by cancer had written. Whether in the raw, searching of a writer such as Sharon Carr or the light-handed depth of Bill Zimmerman's books, a theme began to emerge—a theme that articulated the intensity of the beauty of the whole cycle of life—light and darkness, joy and pain, birth and death.

I began to trust my own experience as life unfolded on a deeper, more intuitive level.

We are fortunate in Richmond to have a place, the Hawthorne Cancer Center, where cancer survivors come together. It is not a place of treatment, but a place of replenishment—a beautiful, relaxing series of rooms with fresh flowers, colorful fish tanks, soft sofas—a place just to hang out. There I met some of the most caring, honest, brave persons I have ever known. As I shared my jottings with these persons, they shared their thoughts and longings with me. As well as our backgrounds, there was a wide difference in our individual responses to cancer. While not consistent, our shared experiences were enlightening and comforting. We shared times of honesty, compassion, crying, calmness, and yes, even laughter and joy.

I longed for just such an experience in our local churches, and with very little effort, I found it. Two Christian educators allowed me to lead such a group in their churches. The members of the class just seemed to emerge. It convinced me that persons are here, in our local churches, waiting for such an opportunity to join in this incredible learning experience, to minister and be ministered unto.

Since then, I have taught other classes. Some of the class members have since died, some have been pronounced "cancer free," some have experienced a recurrence of their cancer, and some are in remission. Wherever they are on their journey, I hope they feel as blessed as I do for the time we shared together seeking to learn from our cancer.

Prologue

This book is for cancer survivors. In our society the power of modern medicine is making us cautiously optimistic of longer ongoing cancer survival. There are more of us than ever in the long-term survivor situation and our expectations for continuing as such are high.

According to the Centers for Disease Control and the National Cancer Institute, there are currently 10.5 million cancer survivors living in the United States, and will be an anticipated 20 million by the year 2015. Breakthroughs in new treatments and cures, being announced almost daily, will add to this number of survivors. Every congregation has been touched in one way or another by this scourge. How have we, the church, responded? In one of two ways.

First, some churches have cancer support groups that exist for fellowship and friendship. A leader in one such group said to me, "We just want to fill ourselves with uplifting discussions and stay on light subjects. The subject of death and dying came up the other night and none of us wanted to focus on that. Our focus seems to be on celebrating recovery." Second, on the other end of the spectrum, some churches have persons to help during the last stages of a cancer patient's life. There seems to be a void between these two perspectives. This book is an attempt to fill that void.

Cancer happens in the body, and yet can profoundly affect the soul. When the body is ailing, questions arise about the meaning of life, why we are here, and who and what really matters. Cancer forces us to ask basic questions about life and death. We are in "liminal" time. ("Liminal" comes from the Latin word for "threshold.") Thresholds and crises are unavoidable. They can be unbearable unless we work them into a larger framework of life. These are certainly issues to which the church can speak. Should we not have groups within our churches to help cancer survivors in their search for understanding?

The spiritual needs of cancer survivors are unique. Pastors, lay persons, and even care-givers, though wanting desperately to be of help, may not be able to speak authentically to these needs. Those who have traveled this road can understand more completely. I know this sounds elitist, but I believe it to be true.

There should be a place in the church where cancer survivors come together to seek to understand what this episode in their lives was/is all about. We need a community where we can try to make sense of hard pain. Such a group brings together meaning, hope, and vision. We seek to understand what we are going through. Some persons hesitate to attend such a group because cancer is a fearful subject to them. What they may find is that other survivors have experienced these same questions and fears. We need a place where it is OK to doubt, to shake our fists at God, to ponder Scripture for our own interpretation, to think about passages again and again until we can penetrate clearly into what, for us, is reality. We want to connect this concrete experience in our lives to the intangibles that guide our living.

Though the outcome of such personal searching has been, in my experience, a deeper, more vibrant faith (you can read testimonies from actual cancer survivors in this book), it has only come about through honest, unblinking looks at ourselves. The poet Robert Frost said, "The best way out is always through." That is what we have bypassed in the church—the hard road, the dark tunnel with no light in sight, the time of trudging on. It is in these times that we incorporate into our lives the impact of our present experience as well as the wisdom of a backward look.

A variation of these pages was experienced with cancer survivors in a variety of different settings: a retreat of Christian educators, a cancer center connected to a local hospital, and in two different congregational settings. This book is a result of those classes as well as my own struggle with cancer.

Whether you are just beginning your cancer journey or are several years in remission, there is much you can learn about yourself from this powerful turning point in your life. Learning does not just mean to receive information; it also means to cut through misconceptions and have insights and "ah-ha" moments of understanding. Cancer brings blessings, hardships, and teachings. We can immediately list the hardships. Blessings are a little harder to see at first, and teachings are perhaps the hardest of all. We may wish just to forget this whole experience, but when all that cancer survivors go through is forgotten, nothing is learned.

The first section of this book, the Workbook, is for the facing of this life-changing experience in your particular life. It was designed for use as a six-week study in a group setting, but you may also use it as an individual at your own pace. Narratives from other cancer survivors are included for your consideration. You will work through your cancer history to a point where you can gain a new sense of self in this changed circumstance. The quest for wholeness and new meaning begins. You will go deeply into your feelings and will connect this cancer experience with the rest of your life. There are questions to help you explore how you feel; art activities to get at intuitive learning; assignments to stretch your comfort level; Scripture to adopt or refute. All of these activities are tools for inner exploration.

Though this workbook may be used privately "for survivor's eyes only," it is my hope that churches will form survivor groups to explore this study together. The second section of the book is particularly for those persons who will be starting a cancer survivor group in a local church or other setting. If you are doing this workbook on your own, you may still find the supplementary material here helpful. This section of the book seeks to affirm that the church has a beneficial role to play both in improving how people cope with cancer and in facilitating recovery.

SECTION I

Workbook

CHAPTER 1
Watering the Seeds of Happiness with Cancer

Welcome! You are a cancer survivor! Whether you have just received your diagnosis of cancer or have been in remission many years—you are a survivor.

You have had a unique experience, and your life will never be the same again. Your challenge is to integrate this experience into your life. In Chinese, the hexagram for "opportunity" and "crisis" is the same. You have been given a powerful opportunity to learn about yourself. Cancer doesn't allow you to live superficially. You can use this phase of your life as a challenge to grow and find personal meaning and spiritual strength. You may find self-realization and an intensification of the inner life. From an early age you *know* you are going to die. With cancer you are *aware* of it, and that is a great difference. St. Ignatius called it "tasting and feeling the truth"—not just knowing it, but tasting and feeling it. The difference is between information and awareness. By living this experience and pondering it, we can make some sort of sense of the upheavals and suffering.

Some people looking at Jesus once asked, "Can anything good come out of Nazareth?" We are going to ask, "Can anything good come out of cancer?" How does God figure into what is happening to me? We have the opportunity to deal with ultimate questions such as: Where is God in all this? If you pay attention, you can find much that is useful and inspiring, even through cancer. You will discover various deeper dimensions of yourself.

This workbook is just for you—to ponder, to reflect upon, to consider your unique life journey. In each of the chapters we will explore some learning points. This workbook will not give you black and white answers but something better—an opportunity to explore your uniqueness and find your individual access to God even through this experience. There are questions you may never answer, but the catharsis is in the asking. Each chapter will give you the opportunity to probe your values and clarify your thoughts. You will read what other survivors going through a similar experience have written and will have the opportunity to agree or disagree. Although cancer is something we must face alone, it is helpful to consider how others have dealt with those times when we run into rough spots or lose heart. Knowing that others have had similar experiences helps. They offer us words from someone familiar with the territory, images, and metaphors.

It takes courage to learn about yourself, but it is well worth the risk.

Are you ready to begin? Today we will forget the needles and the pain and the nausea and begin to lay the foundation for dealing with cancer in our lives. Learning point 1:

You are more than your Cancer.
It is only one part of who you are.

As we consider this point, we find comfort in the Scripture passage:

Isaiah 61:1. You may recognize this first part—"The Spirit of the Lord is upon me." These were the words Jesus read in the synagogue as he began his ministry. As he continued his reading he might have been speaking to cancer patients.

> To comfort all who mourn and provide for those who mourn in Zion.
> To give them a garland instead of ashes,
> The oil of gladness instead of mourning,
> The mantle of praise instead of a faint spirit.
> They will be called Oaks of Righteousness, the planting of the LORD
> to display his splendor. Isaiah 61:2b-4

Consider this phrase: "Oaks of Righteousness." Through this cancer experience we are called to be oaks! Our faith gives us symbols on which to lean. Let your mind rest in the metaphor of an oak tree. Oak wood is hard, tough, and durable. Two important English legendary figures are associated with the oak— King Arthur, who gathered his knights around an oak round table, and Robin Hood, who lived among the oak trees of Sherwood Forest. These figures embody two sides of oak lore—caring, paternal qualities and the ability to fight ruthlessly when justice demanded it. Both of these qualities can help us in our battle with cancer.

LIFELINE NO. 45
Never lose sight of what is special about you

Continuing to use this image consider your whole life. You are so much more than your cancer. No one has ever lived your life before and no one will live it again. You are unique. Let us consider the unique Oak of Righteousness you are called to be.

Look at the illustration below. Now turn to page 25 and on the trunk there, write your name. On the roots, write your religious roots. What is your background? Churched? Unchurched? What about your parents? Write their names in. How strong were these roots in your life? On other roots, name your environment. Where were you raised? Jill Conway in her book *The Road from Coorain* says the environment shapes your worldview and your predominant myths. Ponder this statement in relation to your life.

Nature has a subtle, profound effect on us. More perhaps than we realize. In what environment did you spend most of your life, and how has it affected you? For example: some view an ocean environment as cold and frightening. Others associate it with vacation and fun. Some love the mountains and see their vistas as inspiring. Others view the mountains as smothering. As you write, ponder how the landscape may have affected your spiritual life. Do you see the world as threatening? Harsh? Beautiful? Predictable? Do any of these feelings relate to your environment? Take as long as you want to ponder who you are—a unique tree, reaching for the light, gaining strength from the darkness at your roots. Our roots are our deep selves.

At the ground around your roots scatter some acorns. Acorns are symbols of possibilities. Just as the future of an oak tree is encoded in the acorn, so too has your future been encoded in your roots and all the innumerable events of your past and present. On some of your acorns write the dreams you had as a child or your parent's dreams for you. Consider in your life where the "potential" was made "actual" and how this has affected who you are now.

Looking at oak trees, we do not see a straight line from root to branches. Trees contain notches and burls and galls. So do our lives. Add these now to your tree on p. 25. Reflect on the changes in your life as you grew up. Death of a parent? Moving to a new community? Change in family finances? Add notches that were turning points in your life. Where did you take risks? Where were you wounded as you grew? What things outside of your control changed your life? Wounding makes us stop, shift in new directions. Where do you see this in your life? Though we are never completely healed of the wounds, they can deepen our growth, just as burls add beauty to an oak tree. The trunk of a tree is the conduit of our life force. Focus on prominent curves and knots. Your trunk is strong and you have survived.

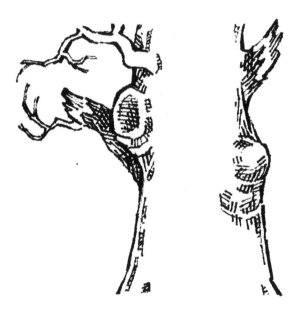

Now move up the tree and add branches and fruit. (I know, oaks don't have fruit as such, but your life does, so your tree will reflect that!) Reflect now on your achievements. We tend to emphasize the rough places in our lives and do a great injustice to ourselves. Name each fruit with something you have achieved or some good you have done or that has been done through you. Take as long as you want. These fruits represent the blossoming of potential into full fruition.

Our tree also has broken branches. Add these now as you reflect on the failures and losses in your life. It might be the loss of youth, or friends, or opportunities. There is no life that has not had failures and losses. Reflect on your losses and how these have affected you.

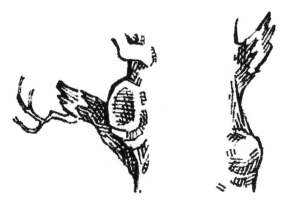

Finally, our tree has some falling leaves. Decay is inevitable. Leaves remind us, as they cling precariously to the bough, how fleeting beauty is. Appreciation of this fleeting beauty can enrich us. As you add these falling leaves to your tree on p. 25, label each leaf with words you would like to have said about you or beauty that you have seen in your life.

Now consider your unique tree. An oak exemplifies nobility, endurance, and strength. You, as a cancer survivor, embody all three.

Take as long as you like to meditate on this Oak of Righteousness, which is yourself. Your tree may be located in a dark, dense wood right now. But like a tree reaching for the light, you stand. Your trunk may be twisted by a storm right now, yet in your uniqueness you are beautiful—an Oak of Righteousness. Look again at your tree.

This is your life with its history and its future—with its shortcomings and with its possibilities. This is your life, which God accepts in grace and fills with his love.

Unique in God's forest, loved and cherished by God, thankful to God for the gift of your distinctive life, we move to another learning point.

We all have happy memories that we can access.

Illness sometimes produces a feeling of becoming a non-self. You looked at how you are unique from every other person. Now take your uniqueness a step further. You have individual memories that are yours alone. They are like hidden gold. As you mine those memories they can define and affirm you.

If you allow it, sickness can gradually open the mind to a world of simple wonders that you may have forgotten since early childhood. You need to get in touch with this childhood wonder to strengthen your foundations as you move through cancer. The child you once were remains within.

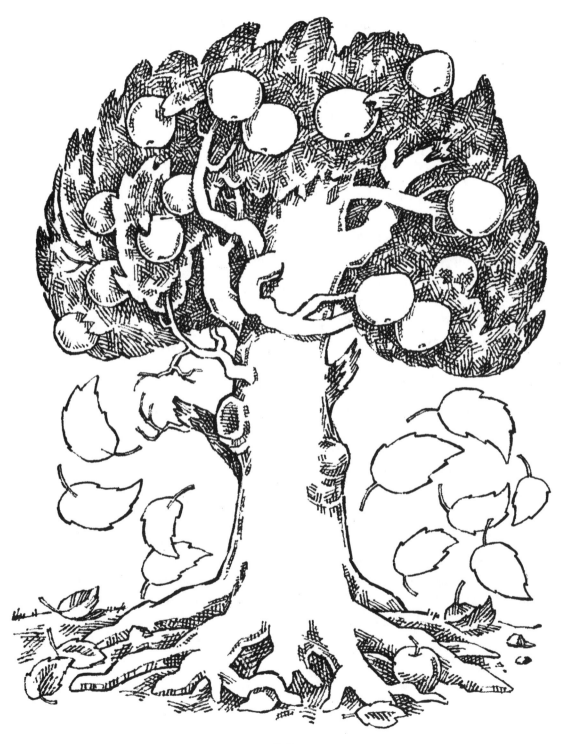

There was a time for all of us when each day was fresh and new, when we looked with wonder and curiosity at each new thing that crossed our path. Observe a young child and you will learn much. As you watch, try to get in touch with your own child-self.

Let your breathing help you.

Sit quietly and become aware of your breath. Then, on each in-breath, recall the earliest thought of yourself that you can remember. Breathe in yourself at four or five years of age. As you breathe out, *smile*. Go again to that innocent, vulnerable, trusting child that was you. Stay with your breathing in this manner for a while.

Now, recall a happy childhood memory.

Some jump-start questions may be: Whom did you play with? What games did you play? Did you have a pet? Think of casting a net and gathering a happy childhood memory. Picture in your mind that experience of childhood happiness. Recall details. Where were you? With whom? And what was it that elicited this happy feeling? Remember as vividly as you can. Create the scene in your mind. Put yourself right there. Feel those emotions again. Relive it all. Try to remember the senses—what did you see, hear, smell, taste, or touch? If you were smiling or laughing, just recall how wonderful it was to be in that warm and healthy, positive and open state. Allow yourself to feel the happiness as completely as you can

We know that a positive attitude can work for us in our healing. Good times as well as bad need definition and incorporation into our whole self.

Finally, let go of that mental picture without losing awareness of the feeling state. As memory slips away, continue to be happy. Rest peacefully in this wholesome feeling state. This is healthy energy to bring to your daily activities. Jot down in this space a word or paragraph that will help you recall these memories so that you can go again and again to this place. Or, gather up old photographs from a happy childhood experience. Place them here if you like as a reminder of happy times. This can help you diminish the all-consuming nature of cancer.

_____

_____

_____

_____

_____

_____

_____

It is interesting that for most people when they look back, the simple things become significant. The happiest memories seem to be of small wonders rather than actions or achievements. In these ordinary details life is savored. When a class of cancer survivors was asked to recall a happy childhood memory they responded:

> I remember sleeping in a cold room upstairs during the winter and running down the steps to gather around the pot belly stove to change clothes for school. Then begin our walk up the street and through the lumber yard for a short cut to school.—Jackie Matze

Jackie also remembered: "My sister Ruth and I would take two straight pins, cross them and place them on the train track so the train would run over them and make us little scissors."

Jewell English wrote:

> When I was seven, I received a small tea set that was just perfect for my three dolls and me to have tea. Dressed in their finest out-fits, my dolls were placed on makeshift chairs around a wooden table under our lofty pecan tree. My mother gave me the used tea leaves so I was able to serve real tea to my dolls and me. We had fine tea cakes with rich icing that existed only in my imagination. As we drank our tea there was a lively conversation around the table. It was my chance to teach my dolls proper manners. We never seemed to tire of our tea parties.

Jo remembered getting one toy for Christmas and what joy it gave her. Sara Jo remembered a day that was so hot, her family went to the movies and sat through two movies in one day just to enjoy the air-conditioning. Ann had memories of vacations at the beach. Elaine wrote of the joy of raspberries and cream and Fay recalled the cinnamon smell that was always present in her grandmother's kitchen. The memories were each unique and of simple things. Jean said: "We were poor and did not even know it."

LIFELINE NO. 1
You will be all right if you think of beauty

Reliving happy memories are an important part of our healing. They are a balm. You might want to keep a happy memories journal. Memory is a powerful thing, a wonderful gift, for in remembering we do more than recall past events. In a sense we bring them into the present and find they nurture us here and now. We remember the person we once were and who still persists in our minds. Bathing a numbed heart in good feelings can heal wounds and restore a sense of being fully alive.

The Lifelines that appear in your workbook are from *Lifelines, A Book of Hope* by William Zimmerman. These thoughts were written during the time of his brother's death "as a way to come to terms with my grief and to create some meaning from the ashes of my pain." *Lifelines, A Book of Hope* is a collection of helping thoughts that offer comfort and hope to "the child in each of us to get us through our lonely nights."

Remind yourself of what has given you warmth and comfort. Surround yourself with these memories. Let them soothe and refresh you. Flood yourself with as many beautiful memories as you can. Think of all the beauties you have seen: flowers, trees, stars at night, and faces of loved ones. Remember beautiful sounds: music, song of birds, and human voice. In gratitude, recall smells, touches, tastes. For now, bask in your happy memories. Remember that although you have cancer, it is only one part of your life. You can affirm and build on your happy memories. They are a good foundation. No matter how much of your past is no longer available, there are always additional memories to retrieve.

Now is the time to do it. Like money saved for a rainy day we may have been hoarding these memories. Maybe someone told you not to live in the past. Nonsense! This is the time to cash in—to call forth those memories. You lived through those happy times—claim them. These memories are a gift, unique to you alone.

But like all good things, the reward is in how you use it.

Don't—**do not**—wallow in the fact that these times of happy memory are gone. Don't let memories make you sad. Instead, rejoice that this was once a part of your life, and through concentration and imagination, you can go there again. You can stay with those memories until you feel the emotions you felt then. You can go back there, back to a time when each day shone with a golden glow. There are times when you must honor the past. Lifeline No. 37 says, "Recall all the good times. They are so much better than the bad ones."

CHAPTER 2

Beautiful Images with Cancer

Something important is happening, and you are invited to notice and pay attention. You have been monitoring from the outside what is happening to you. You have looked inward and begun to recall your memories, to relive and experience again a happy moment from childhood. You learned that cancer is only one part of your life. You are unique and loved by God. This can serve as a good foundation. With this as background we move to our next discovery.

All good times are not in the past.

We are surrounded by everyday epiphanies. To get in the habit of encountering them, look each day for two things:

Something that surprises you
Something that inspires you

Many of us blunder through our lives as though we were asleep. Just being deliberately focused on seeing makes you more alert, more excited, more optimistic. You look, listen, and expect a life-giving surprise. Daily lives are transformed into expectation of meaningful sights. You may see things you have never noticed before.

In the following chart, under each day this week, write what you saw that was a surprise and what you saw that was an inspiration.

Monday   Surprise _____ Inspire _____

Tuesday   Surprise _____ Inspire _____

Wednesday   Surprise _____ Inspire _____

Thursday   Surprise _____ Inspire _____

Friday   Surprise _____ Inspire _____

Saturday   Surprise _____ Inspire _____

Sunday   Surprise _____ Inspire _____

In a class of cancer survivors these surprises were experienced:

One student in the class was shocked by seeing a dead kangaroo on the side of the road. A kangaroo? In Richmond, Virginia? Now, that is a surprise! Discovering later that there was a farm of exotic animals nearby, and that that particular stretch of highway was crowded with cars and frequent road kill did not lessen the impact of the surprise. Perhaps if he had not been looking intently he wouldn't have noticed. Knowing you are going to write it down makes you more observant.

Fresh eyes looking at nature was the source of surprises and inspirations for some in the class. One student, seeing the mud after a rain was reminded of the Genesis story that we are all made from the clay of the earth and she found inspiration in the insight that we are a part of nature.

A member of the class who was attending by email wrote:

> My family doctor never ceases to amaze me. On my last visit to his office, he surprised me when he said he would come to my house when I needed him to call. Last week he came to my house to check me over as getting about is very difficult now. He will come this week also. Compassion is alive and well!—Jewell

Deliberately looking makes you more observant. There is an added acuteness to vision.

One student found inspiration seeing the sunlight on her granddaughter's auburn hair—a precious everyday moment in her life, as if seen for the first time.

LIFELINE NO. 17

Look for the flowers the bright colors in you. They are there waiting to be picked.

Most of us are gifted with sight. Imagine yourself blind. There is much magic remaining in the world just waiting to be seen. What would you want to see if you were seeing for the first time? Perhaps you would look first at the people whose kindness, gentleness, and companionship make life worth living for you. Or perhaps you would wish to take a long walk looking at the beauties of nature in the woods or by a sea shore, trying desperately to absorb the vast splendor constantly unfolding. Would you choose to watch the sunrise and sunset as your first sight?

Looking is good, but now we go a little deeper. An interesting thing to consider is this:

What makes the difference is not the event, but the eyes through which it is seen.

Look again at what happened to you this week. Thousands of thoughts float through your mind every day. Awareness exercises such as looking for surprises and inspiration make you conscious of precious everyday moments in your life. It can make you realize how much magic remains in the world just waiting to be discovered.

To repeat: What makes the difference is not the event, but the eyes through which it is seen.

Think about what things attracted your attention. The skeleton of your true self is emerging. This is when you start learning things about yourself. Why were you attracted to the particular object or thought on which you focused? When you write down what you see, you are also writing about what you are *choosing* to see.

Study your list of what you chose to see this week and see if there are any patterns, any insight. Look for indications of what attracted you. Look for a theme. For example, look at what you put down under "inspiration." There should be seven items, one for each day in the week. How many came:

> From nature?
> From something you read?
> From some person?

Where do you most often find inspiration?

> If it is a person—is it more often the same person?
> Is there any pattern?
> And where do you find surprises?
> What startles you awake?

Knowing where you find inspiration and surprises, you can choose to accent them.

Whatever we pay attention to will grow. This may tell you where your attention needs to shift. You can accent these moments of surprise and inspiration.

Whatever we pay attention to will grow.

Surprises and inspiration are all around us. By slowing us down, cancer can make us more aware. Some cancer survivors found inspiration in:

> nature
>
> books

newspaper

music

brochures on cancer

TV

We discover that the biggest roadblock to our awareness of surprises and inspiration is our agenda. We can become distracted from beauty and wonder by human preoccupations with the nitty-gritty.

It is also difficult to focus if we are encrusted with our own pain. Intentionally being aware helps return some degree of stability to our rocky lives, even when we are experiencing hard pain.

WHAT YOU SEE IS WHAT YOU GET

What you choose to see says a lot about who you are.

Consider Philippians 4:8:

> Finally brothers, whatever is true, whatever is honorable, whatever is just whatever is pure, whatever is pleasing whatever is commendable—if there is any excellence and if there is anything worthy of praise—think about these things.

After reflecting on this verse, take the opposite of each of these traits. Thinking back over the past 24 hours: Did your mind dwell on ignoble things? Wrong things? Impure things? Ugly things? These thoughts are equally available to you. It's your choice.

You have looked for surprises and inspiration; now look for these traits illuminated for us by Saint Paul. They are all around you if you have eyes to see. What do you see?

_____

_____

_____

Poets seem to have a gift for seeing, and poetry is their medium. Poetry is something hard to define, but we'll define poetry as "an overflowing of powerful feelings recollected in tranquility." This is also a description of our reflections on cancer.

Fay Austin wrote a poem, "Twelve Ways of Seeing a Sea Shell" in which she lists twelve different things or scenes she sees when she looks at a conch shell. Look carefully at this picture. Imagine the colors: the graduating shades of pink, the pearl tone.

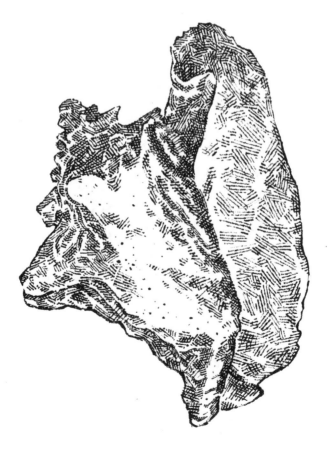

Now read the following poem, one line at a time. Shut your eyes, and then, between lines, open your eyes and try to see what the author suggests.

> The opening of a calla lily
>
> A fountain spout
>
> The face of a small giraffe
>
> The metamorphosis of a rainbow into a butterfly
>
> Sun glistened sand dunes
>
> An emerging snail
>
> A water slide
>
> Scuba divers nook
>
> A wave curling its way to the shoreline
>
> The ear of an elephant
>
> A coral reef
>
> Turtle feet

How many images could you see? Which was your favorite?

Now look at this picture of an artichoke.

Using your imagination, try to see this object in another way. See if you can come up with 12 ways to view an artichoke. A response from one cancer survivor was "petals of hope."

1.

2.

3.

4.

5.

6.

7.

8.

9.

10.

11.

12.

Objects remain the same, but you change your viewpoint. You now view the world from the perspective of the miraculous. A new point of view, a different perspective, is a gift cancer brings to us if we allow it. Iris Murdock said, "People from a planet without flowers would think we must be mad with joy the whole time to have such things about us."

WALKING MEDITATIONS

If you are able, try a walking meditation. Although we walk all the time, a walking meditation is different. Any location is good, even a hospital corridor, but, if possible walk in some beautiful place. The point is not to arrive at any specific destination, nor it is to increase your heart rate. Just walk and enjoy each step. Your pace is a little slower than your normal walk. Breathe deeply and co-ordinate your breathing with your steps. Recall a beloved hymn and let the rhythm of the hymn synchronize walking. A hymn like "Great Is Thy Faithfulness" works well, and can offer strong affirmations to cancer patients. With the rhythm of your steps you can repeat over and over "All I have needed, Thy hand has provided. Great Is Thy Faithfulness, Lord unto me." This becomes a walking prayer of praise. Walk with gentleness. Walk with joy. Walk in the Spirit. Maybe during your walk you will see something inspiring, something surprising, refreshing your mind and body. If you wish, imagine every step makes a flower bloom under your feet. The English poet Christina Rossetti said, "Tread softly, all the earth is holy ground." Let go of fearful thoughts of the past and future. Become aware that life can only be found in the present moment.

LIFELINE NO. 33

Your imagination is stronger than your fears will ever be

Instead of a hymn you may find a Scripture passage strengthening for you as you walk.

Consider Isaiah 40:31:

> Those who wait for the LORD
> Shall Renew their Strength
> They Shall Mount Up with Wings like Eagles
> They Shall Run and Not Be Weary
> They Will Walk and Not Faint

CHAPTER 3
Open Doors with Cancer

No one really expects to be diagnosed with cancer, but for each of you *there came a moment* when you heard the words "You have cancer." It was the dreaded "C" word that carries such foreboding. Life took a different turn and you were gathered up into a whole different way of seeing and being. This is the moment you are going to return to now. Try to relive it and seek wisdom about yourself.

Though you share much in common with other cancer survivors, though there is universality to the cancer chronicle, every person's account is distinct.

Confront your own story—how was it for you when you were first diagnosed? This was a significant event and you need to gauge its impact in your life. You have already affirmed that cancer isn't all there is to life. There are pleasures in past memories and present awareness but to overcome the suffering cancer brings, you must face it squarely.

What can you learn from this moment, the moment you first heard your diagnosis?

We will honor the path of this moment by reflecting on it. Reflection is the first step in making sense. All of us have different backgrounds, different tolerances for pain, different family situations, different resources, and we react in different ways. There is no right or wrong way to respond to a diagnosis of cancer.

There is only *your* way. You will look at how you did respond at the moment you heard the news that you had cancer.

Whirlwinds of feelings occur for most survivors when you first receive your diagnosis. Take the feelings apart and look at them. There is often *fear*. Fear of cancer is instilled in many of us from an early age. The word "cancer" is often equated with death. It is attended by anxiety and depression as often as by courage and dignity. In spite of how informed we may be, a diagnosis of cancer is always a *shock*. Shock is often accompanied by a sense of being lost and out-of-control. "While the surgeon spoke, I listened, numbly." one survivor said. *Numbness* is another typical reaction. We are stunned and without words for the depth into which we are plunged. Here is how some other survivors received the news of their cancer.

> Life has changed. We have been attacked—without warning. On a day when the sky was blue and everyone went about their daily business—life was interrupted. The unthinkable had happened. Fear began. The rest of the world goes on but there is still a lump in our throats and tears in our eyes. What about our loved ones? Will they be okay? Will I be okay? What does the future hold? Nothing is the same. Suddenly priorities change. The pettiness is so silly. The prayers are so sincere. No, it's not terrorism, it's cancer. Welcome to our world.—Cindy Smith

> The gravity of my situation hit me at a vulnerable time. I was on a surgical table having what I'd been told was a benign lump removed. Although fully awake I was a little groggy from a pre-op shot of valium. I heard my surgeon say, "I don't like the looks of this"—and I knew. When they rolled me in a wheelchair a little later into a private office my husband was sitting there looking like a deer in the headlights. We were given the diagnosis of malignancy (the tissue had already been checked downstairs) and we listened as my doctor called to schedule an operating room. He said it would be a week before we could have the surgery done, and

my husband got excited and said we must do it immediately before the cancer had a chance to spread any more. Finally the doctor convinced him that a week would not matter—and we went home to endure what we would later refer to as "the hard time."

During that week we attended church and that was when I found my peace with the situation. I could not presume to ask for a cure, when so many were not cured, but I felt justified in asking for strength to cope—and I did receive that. Although not free of fear (whoever is?) I felt strengthened and comforted throughout my surgery and recovery. I am grateful to God—and to my husband, who was, and continues to be, my "soft place to fall."—Pat Broaddus

I will never forget the gulp
That meant the end of my dreams
And the start of Your meaning.—Sharon Carr, from *Life was a Triumph*

Fear. Shock. Numbness. How can we live in this new baffling and uncertain world? Recalling and reflecting give us permission to explore the ocean of mystery cancer presents. However, rehashing the time of impact can be *either* good *or* bad.

What is good about it? What is the value of telling our story again and again?

It is *good* to get it out of your system, to be vulnerable in your grief, to want compassion and understanding and to reach out for nurturing when you are afraid.

What is *bad* about it? What is dangerous about telling our cancer story? **We can get stuck in the story.** It is *bad* to wallow in your cancer story, to indulge in feeling victimized and to tell your story just for the purpose of soliciting sympathy.

Think on these things—the good and bad of telling our cancer story to others. With which do you identify?

LIFELINE NO. 44

You are much stronger than you realize
Know that jitters belong only
In a jitter bag, not within yourself

Those of us who have experienced cancer know the truth of these raw statements made by other survivors. Externalizing the myriad of feelings that are triggered with the impact of a diagnosis of cancer can bring insight and objectivity to a situation that typically feels overwhelming. Did familiar feelings surface in you as you read the survivor's responses?

These were the experiences of others. Now let your own feelings, thoughts, and energies come up. Explore the full range of your emotions. One of the characteristics common to many cancer patients is that they are not very expressive of their feelings. They tend to keep deep sentiments of anger, fear, and resentment to themselves. Just as you can't deal with cancer you haven't detected, so you can't get rid of negative feelings until you recognize them. Admit your lugubrious feelings. Accept cancer's reality in your life.

Use imagery to help you deal with your feelings. Start to envision your feelings as a swarm of bees buzzing around your head, creating a constant background noise of vague anxiety. Imagine each of these negative feelings as a bee. Draw them and name them. This one is "fear." This one "self-pity." Here is "nameless panic." This one is the "frightening unknown." Here is "woundedness." This bee is named "sadness." This one, "depression." Add others of your own.

Then, mentally guide the bees one by one safely into a beehive. They have gone away to a place where they cannot cause any trouble. The buzzing becomes a little quieter. Inside the beehive are security and golden honey and sweetness. Think of the honey as your awareness of the divine. Meditate on

Psalm 118:12 "They swarmed around me like bees, but they died out as quickly as burning thorns in the name of the LORD I cut them off." (NIV) Consider the waste of energy to maintain all that complexity of feelings. Admit your feelings—bring them to the fore. Get them out of your system. It is only by expressing all that is within you that purer and purer honey comes into awareness.

Add one last bee: "*Hope*." We need hope in the midst of the swarm of our emotions. In the absence of certainty we hold on to hope. Fear and other anxieties are natural responses. But you can move beyond fear to trust in God's love for you. We pray, "Lord, instill in me a reason for hope. Calm the buzzing bees."

Another help in calming our negative emotions is to read the book of Psalms. It is a potent force for dealing with your feelings. As we read, we become vividly aware that life holds joy and despair in the same hand. For your comfort, meditate on passages that speak most vividly to you of God's tenderness. For example:

> And now O LORD What do I wait for?
> My hope is in You
> Hear my prayer, O Lord,
> And give ear to my cry. Psalm 39:7,12

> Answer me when I call, O God of my right!
> You gave me room when I was in distress.
> Be gracious to me, and hear my prayer. Psalm 4:1

> God is our refuge and strength,
> A very present help in trouble.
> Therefore we will not fear,
> though the earth should change,
> though the mountains shake in the heart of the sea; though its waters roar and foam,
> the mountains tremble with its tumult. (Psalm 46:1-3)

And don't forget the 23rd Psalm. It is so well-known that sometimes our eyes race over the well-known phrases and much may be missed. Go over these familiar words and find new depth at this juncture in your life.

> The Lord is my shepherd, I shall not want.
> He makes me lie down in green pastures;
> He leads me beside still waters;
> He restores my soul.
> He leads me in right paths
> For his name's sake.
> Even though I walk through the darkest valley,
> I fear no evil;
> For you are with me;

Your rod and your staff—
They comfort me.
You prepare a table before me
In the presence of my enemies; you anoint my head with oil;
My cup overflows.
Surely goodness and mercy
Shall follow me
All the days of my life,
And I shall dwell in the house of
The Lord
My whole life long. Psalm 23

Now move from imagery to the concrete world through three dialogues. In **diaglogue one**, go back directly to that time with your doctor when you learned you had cancer. Remember as exactly as you can what was said. Remember where you were—how it sounded—how it looked and smelled and what your reaction was. Some survivors received the news over the telephone and when alone. Others had personal visits to their homes from their doctor. There are all gradations of doctors' manners. By whatever method, there is potentially stunning power in a doctor's words. Relive the situation when you received your diagnosis. As nearly as you can, remember the exact conversation. Record it here.

The doctor said _____

I said _____

Then the doctor said _____
Continue this conversation.

_____

_____

_____

Patients are often confused by the increasing number of options open to them. I heard the story of one woman with breast cancer who was given so many options (Chemo or no chemo? Lumpectomy or mastectomy? Radiation or not?) that she became distraught and told her family she was going to get a bumper sticker saying "Honk if you think I should have a lumpectomy."

Now look for insight in your response to your doctor. Observe any tendency to apologize, dramatize, or retreat into denial. Was there any blame? Be honest with yourself. Don't let anyone tell you how you should have responded. Look clear-eyed at how you *did* respond. Were you just silent? Did you look away or avoid eye contact? Or did you confront your doctor head on, asking questions? Did you try to find out all you could about your diagnosis? Each has an individual threshold of "readiness to learn."

Some of us want to know all the facts of our disease, others want the barest minimum. Which describes you? Apply this to your particular cancer situation, your sensitivity to the way the news of your cancer was conveyed. Consider your response. When you are in the midst of a situation, you don't have the advantage of perspective—You are just in it. Recall and observe as an outsider might do. Don't be hard on yourself or judge yourself in any way. Now, from a distance, consider that experience and what you will do with it.

You have looked as clearly as you can remember at how you responded to your cancer diagnosis; look now at a second dialogue.

In our **second dialogue** we'll look at the same situation but, as though it was happening to someone else. We'll "try on" someone else's response in order to better understand our own. This time, we don't personalize what is happening. Make your response as indicated below. Here is the situation: You tell your children, parents, or a close friend about your just-received diagnosis. Following are a number of ways to tell this news. Do a bit of acting. Drama is "feeling out loud." Your perception of truth comes through the intensity of imagination. If the situation makes it possible, just let yourself go—*overact*—get into the responses.

1. Try telling this news as *dramatically* as you can. For example you might say, "The most terrible thing possible has happened to me!" "No one has *ever* had anything this terrible happen to

them." Overplay it until it becomes ridiculous. Improvise your dialogue.

2. Respond with an *apology.* "I am so sorry I am doing this to you." For example, "I know we had planned a trip for this summer. Now I have just spoiled everything,"—etc.

3. Respond with *denial.* "I know this isn't true—the tests were wrong. I feel too good. There is some terrible mistake. I'm just going to ignore it." Think of all the denial reasons you can.

4. Respond with *blame.* "This wouldn't be happening to me if I had been told the dangers of smoking" (working in that chemical plant/ lying in the sun, etc.) ."Why didn't someone tell me? Why didn't *you* tell me?"

5. Respond with *resentment.* "After the good, healthy life I have led, I resent that I was put in a situation where cancer was a danger. I don't deserve this! "

6. Just *laugh it off.* "If I ignore it, it will probably go away. I'll just keep really busy and not worry about it."

7. Respond with *anger.* "I'm furious! I don't have time for this! I may as well get Dr. Kevorkian's phone number." Give your anger full vent.

8. Respond with *guilt.* You may secretly believe you deserve this illness. "I have not lived a very good life and this is my punishment. If I had only . . .", etc.

9. And a very common response: "Why me?" Ask rather: "How do I 'be me' in what is happening?"

Do you recognize yourself in any of these responses? These may not be your responses, but there are elements of each of these in all of us. Here is an opportunity for us to learn about ourselves. Look again at these responses and the negative feelings that were aroused. Did you want sympathy (pity even)?

Attention? Did you want to focus on "me"? Confront any unhealthy pattern. It is the nonjudgmental awareness alone that heals and changes and makes us grow. Study your reactions. What does this say about our way of perceiving the world? Looking at these dialogues raises some interesting questions for you to consider: Do I think it makes me a better person not to show others that I hurt? Is it more Christian to be stoic? Or, on the other hand, do I secretly enjoy the attention I get when I am sick? What is the self I am presenting to the world? Is it the real me?

There is always a danger in taking familiar symptoms of sensations and using them to confirm your suffering. Everyone who has survived cancer has a fear that it might return. We are nagged by every new ache or pain. Hypochondriacs grasp the first sign of discomfort as a clear message that they are seriously ill. Have you been guilty of this? How did you handle it?

There is also power in language. Look at how you refer to yourself. Do you speak about yourself as a victim—a patient—a survivor? Our words can be self-fulfilling prophesies. Become aware of the language you use. Consider death and how we talk about it. Look at the difference between, "I think I am going to die" and, "Death is a part of every life process, and may be the ultimate outcome of this encounter with cancer."

LIFELINE NO 35

Your inner strength can subdue your demons.

Self-talk is the endless stream of thoughts running through your head every day. Critical and negative self-talk can be discouraging. It can put a negative spin on circumstances throughout your life—corroding your attitude perhaps even when things are going well.

Other people can be thoughtless with their words without realizing the impact on a survivor. You may be sensitive to such remarks as, "What *was* your work?" rather than, "What *is* your work?" And though persons mean well, most survivors had rather *not* hear religious clichés and platitudes. such as, "This is God's will" or, "You are going to be just fine." With the nearness of death comes an honesty. There is no refuge in platitudes.

In this **third dialogue**, you are going to have a dialogue with yourself. You will engage in an imaginary conversation with different parts of your psyche. We are composed of many parts. Directly challenge yourself on this question: "Denial or Acceptance—which is braver?" No one can help you here. You listen and argue with yourself.

Imagine two angels sitting on your shoulders. One is Denial and the other is Acceptance. You are going to consider these in relation to your cancer. The Denial angel can be either good or bad. Denial is *good* if you think "I'll fight it!" It is *bad* if you are not facing reality.

Now listen to the angel on your other shoulder, Acceptance. Acceptance is *good* if you think, "This is a part of my life right now and I will accept it." It is *bad* if it makes you think, "I'll just give up."

Such an exercise will encourage you to examine your choices. It will give you objective feedback. Be as honest as you can with yourself. Is that really how I feel? Do I accept this cancer or do I deny it? Why? What can you learn about yourself?

Look at this picture of a knight with sword drawn facing this large, ugly dragon. You are the knight and cancer is the dragon. Using the symbol of a dragon for cancer can represent some intuitive wisdom that eludes direct expression. It may represent all the monstrous devouring elements of the disease. Face the emotions you fear and realize that negative feelings are in *you*, not in reality. Project them onto the dragon. Then using your personal coping methods, confront that dragon. Be bold and brave! Remember, it's not an adventure worth telling if there aren't any dragons.

CHAPTER 4
Hurts that Heal with Cancer

*W*e are beyond the shock and fear of diagnosis now, and in the long, painful stretch of treatments—the time of grinding tedium. If you are currently undergoing treatments, this chapter may offer you helpful suggestions to help you get through it. If you are a long-term survivor, it is good to recall your patience, courage, and endurance during the time of treatment. How you reacted in these situations made you the person you are today. Part of getting over it is knowing you will never get over it. Reflecting on this experience affords clarity and self-empowerment.

During treatment your task is to find a new way of being in the world—a way that includes a loss of energy but still in some ways celebrates life. You are at that "hanging-in" stage. This period requires patience, courage, and endurance.

You are called to let go of plans and desires and abandon yourself to the reality of your condition. Used to measuring value and meaning in terms of actions and achievements, tangible results and immediate relationships, you find yourself in isolation and boredom. Our culture sees sickness as something to be avoided, prevented, or cured.

This period forces you to consider some hard questions: What is the purpose of my life now? Does my life have any value? How do I deal with this pain? Will

I ever be well, in the same sense again? What is the place of pain in a world ruled by a benevolent God?

You turn inward to the quiet and anonymous work of sickness—teaching, testing, challenging and making real your faith. Meditate on Proverbs 17:3 "The crucible is for silver, and the furnace is for gold, but the LORD tests the heart."

This sickness has become an interruption to your life. The world grows accustomed to living without you. You see persons continuing as usual along their life's path and you feel as if you have been pushed off the road and lie in a heap by the roadside as life rushes on. You are off the track of roles, responsibilities, and activities that most people consider significant. While you are sick and others healthy, you just don't fit anywhere in their lives at all. Long illness gradually weans you away from involvement. Hopes fade and plans go unfinished.

LIFELINE NO. 38
You can dream yourself away from all of your hurts

What can you learn as you slog through your treatments? Illness is such a self-centered thing. "When do I take my next medication? How can I get comfortable?" are thoughts that occupy our minds. It helps to look outside ourselves. Move from "I" to "eye." Begin right where you are. What do you *see* around you? Put yourself in the background as an observer instead of the star of this scene. Focus on the particular.

For example, Fay writes:

> "I'm in the waiting room at radiation/oncology. It won't be my turn for a while so instead of reading, I decide to sit and really look at the other patients around me. Someone is working on a puzzle that is on the table to help pass time. I think this is how

she controls her thoughts. She is intent on the pieces she picks up. Maybe she is trying to put the pieces of her life back together. Another person shifts restlessly in her chair watching the door to the treatment area. I think she is anxious to finish her allotted number of treatments and get on with her life. And another person just sits and stares into the space in front of her with a disbelieving gaze, probably at her diagnosis of cancer and her future. Then I realize that all of these people are actually me and that their thoughts, actions, and feelings are mine.

"It has taken me my lifetime to learn to just sit and quietly look at the world around me. I've learned that silence is holy. It draws people together and only those who are comfortable with each other can sit together without speaking. I've also realized what I think is obvious to a child, that life is just a collection of little lives—each one lived one day at a time."—Fay Austin

"With the diagnosis of cancer I found myself centering on my own discomfort. Would I ever be of any use to anyone anymore? Instead of terminal cancer I found myself with terminal despair.

"What moved me beyond this mired condition was not a Paul-like strike of vision, but the awareness of the daily bravery I saw around me in the Infusion Center of our local hospital. I saw nurses, who must have been exhausted from their heavy overload of patients, who were always cheerful. I saw love and patience on the face of caregivers who were sitting quietly and holding the hand of a loved one through long hours of chemical infusion. I saw a man feeble with weakness practicing a foreign language with a tutor, the love of knowledge making his eyes alive with pleasure in a wracked body. I saw patients knitting hats to cover the baldness of others as they themselves were receiving chemotherapy. Wagging friskiness of therapy dogs caused joyful laughter.

"The Center, just a dismal, ugly place was kept bright with donated fresh flowers and home-baked goodies—a decorated tree at Christmas—dyed eggs at Easter. We were all ages, genders, and races who cared about each other. Life and love bloomed in this place through small deeds of kindness. I pray, 'Open my eyes Lord that I may see Thy loving kindness surrounding me and expressed through the deeds of others. Give me perspective and humility.'"—Julia, a cancer survivor

PATIENCE

Just watching and being aware can fill the dead spaces and numbness that comes from long hours of waiting. Cancer offers us endless opportunities in which to practice the art of waiting. Let your breath guide you. The breath is quite seasoned in the art of waiting. Then look outside yourself. The exterior world is filled with interesting things. Observing this world moves you from looking through the cloudy mirror of your own self-reflection to a window on the world.

The waiting itself allows time for reflection. We learn patience as opposed to stress-filled wastes of time, plagued by nervous anticipation and tension. If you are used to your needs being gratified immediately, waiting can be a lesson in patience that cancer teaches you, and a reminder of how patient God is with us. As we learn to wait, we can inch closer to God, who is always present and who waits for us. We can strive to transform our waiting from sheer aggravation to something holy.

Think of a place you associate with your cancer treatment. Do some quick writing—just free association. Consider the five senses. Quickly write down the first word that comes to your mind when you think of a doctor's waiting room or an infusion room. Just one word.

Seeing

Hearing

Touching

Smelling

Tasting

Memory selects the details we might have missed the first time around. Our surroundings can be portals to a realm that transcends the mundane. Now look at the words you wrote to describe the infusion room or waiting room. Were any of your images cold?

Often with cancer we feel a deep sense of cold. Shivering from trauma we are also threatened with inner chill. Our treatments seem like a shocking plunge into winter—a winter that grinds darkly on as we slog through. We need to hollow-out caves of safety within the cold and dark as mountain climbers sometimes hollow-out places of safety in a snow storm.

Since our unconscious mind dwells in images and symbols, try turning these cold thoughts into snowflake imagery. In the crowded, chilled treatment room or doctor's waiting room, let your mind dwell on snowflakes. Nothing is lovelier than a soft, white snowflake, perfectly symmetrical with a wonderful delicacy of form—and it is fleeting.

Similarly, our brief life episodes can be beautiful for all their transience. With a fresh fall of snow, the landscape is changed. So, too, we are walking through a whole new landscape with cancer. Contemplation of snow has a calming effect on the

senses, leaving us with a pervasive peace and confidence that healing is taking place, whether physical or spiritual. Trusting in God, we can know that the warmth and life of Spring will always follow the darkest, coldest winter. God has carried us through the difficulties of past winters in our life. Though now we may be fragile and weakened yet, having obtained the help of God we continue to this day.

LIFELINE NO. 9

There's a time to stop
And
Take stock.
Slowly

Be aware that you can create personal symbols from Nature, such as the snowflake, and draw great strength from these symbols.

ENDURANCE

When your treatments are so harsh and so long, the question of endurance is a very real one. Though each of us has a different tolerance level for pain, physical pain is real. How do you handle suffering and pain? If our reaction is frustration, it is as if we are splintered into a thousand pieces. The more you fight pain, the more power you give it. Concentrate instead, on gathering all your inner resources and accepting the pain, moving into it, breathing with the waves of pain as they wash over you. Feel into the suffering. Be with the pain. The suffering is as real as ever, but the endurance of pain as a negative power is weakened, and pain becomes an accomplishment for the sufferer.

Simple prayers or mantras become helpful here. "Jesus, son of God" as you breathe in; "Have mercy on me" as you breathe out. A mantra is a phrase said over and over. Your mantra may be a strengthening Bible verse or prayer. Whether you say it mindfully or parrot-like without giving attention to the words, reciting gives you the opportunity to exert a little control over your pain. You are in charge of it. It is not in charge of you. Do you have a favorite mantra you could say in times of great pain? Write it here:

_____

_____

_____

_____

You get so weary of pain—of feeling bad and centering life on your symptoms. You may want to draw a spiral of your pain and find yourself on that spiral. Mark the intensity of your pain then travel down the spiral until you are grounded in your mantra.

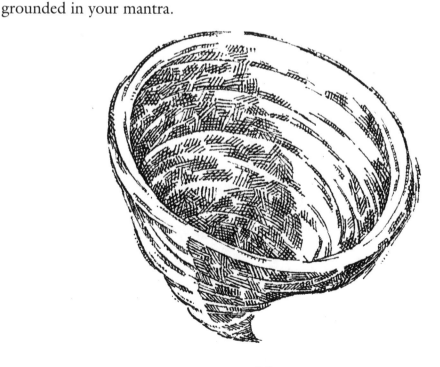

Possibilities lie uniquely in the depth of the lived experience of sickness. Physical pain takes a great deal of our energy and is never an easy thing to bear. Also, tolerance for pain becomes chipped away over the long haul. Pray that God will give strength to the sick and to all who suffer in any way. Pray for strength to bear your pain. Thomas Merton said, "The Christian must not only accept suffering: he must make it holy. Nothing so easily becomes unholy as suffering." It is natural to prefer comfort to pain, but beyond comfort lies grace.

During treatment it sometimes seems as if everyone is making decisions for you. This loss of control can be discouraging. You are a "thing"—a non-person. Think now of ways you can take charge of some aspect of your life at this time. One way to stave off the vulnerability of pain and weariness is to concentrate on what it is of your chores that you can still do. What of normal routine? Fill in this weekly calendar with any mundane task you can still do. For some of you it may be only one thing—a very simple thing. If possible, do this task by yourself to help you feel independent. Can you just fold the weekly laundry? Or dry the dishes? The ordinary task can become a moment free from thoughts of cancer. You become aware of the inherent beauty in the simplest of tasks. Once dreaded household jobs take on the quality of extraordinary ordinariness, and we discover the mystical in the mundane.

Monday   Task _____

Tuesday   Task _____

Wednesday   Task _____

Thursday   Task _____

Friday   Task _____

Saturday   Task _____

Sunday   Task _____

There is such a need in our lives for pattern, routine, and the healing power of simple daily rhythm. Cancer is what it is and as such takes its place in our own cycle of life. There is a time and place to face what is here. And if now you are unable to do anything, remember even your empty days are valuable. Occasionally your task is just to rest and let your psyche rest also. Doing nothing leads you to realize how much of life happens on its own. There is a time to stop and let yourself be surrounded by the healing joys of contentment and rest. The body is tremendously resilient. It bounces back again and again. Reinforce this resilience by appreciating the body's gracious acceptance of your particular treatment. Take one day at a time and let these simple daily tasks be signposts to recovery.

COURAGE

This is also a time to consider courage. At a time of treatment and suffering when you are squeezed, pricked, tested, poked, and cut, you come to affirm that the only kind of courage that matters is the kind that gets you from one moment to the next. The pain may be sharp, the misery deep, but the commitment to another day, or even just another hour, must be made. You have spiritual resources that you may not even know you have. Call on these now.

We have a saying in our family: "'I'm all right so far,' the old man said as he jumped from the seventh-story window." I'm all right *so far*. So are you. In this moment—at this time—you are all right. We may be covered with the scars of many woundings and healings but we are all right—so far. With these words, the threshold and capacity to endure increases. We are able to withstand pain more easily, our hope is not shaken or abandoned however difficult the moment. We are all right at this very moment—so far. And our God is with us.

Sharon Carr expressed this thought powerfully in her poem "Suffering Soldier."

> The danger is having blasts of fear against me and the constant threat wearies me. The stairsteps are growing steeper and steeper and secure footing is harder to sustain. And then You call out to me "Courage and Trust, suffering soldier, in the unflinching railing that is always within your desperate grasp."

CHAPTER 5
Laughing with Cancer

We identify so much with our bodies. We think we are our bodies.
Cancer teaches us that this is not so.

Your body is never the same after cancer. For most there is a new level of tiredness. You learn to live with it. In this chapter you are thinking about what happens to your body, about bodily images, and the effect of cancer on your body. You understand in a new way all those myths about body-changelings, vampires, and werewolves, as you feel and watch your body change.

Am I my body? Science tells us that millions of cells in our body are changed or are renewed every minute so that by the end of seven years we don't have a single, living cell in our body that was there seven years ago. Cells come and cells go. "I" is something other and more than the body.

Try to recall your body image at seven years of age—at 14—at 21—at 28

At seven, I was _____

At 14, I was _____

At 21, I was _____

At 28, I was _____

Continue as needed.

Try to recall what your body structure was like through your whole life over seven-year increments. In so doing, you observe an ever-changing reality.

And what about now? With cancer, you can't cover up your woundedness. You are suddenly exposed. You look in a mirror and don't recognize yourself. Yet Scripture reminds us it was always so.

> There is no soundness in my flesh because of your indignation; there is no health in my bones because of my sin. For my iniquities have gone over my head; they weigh like a burden too heavy for me. My wounds grow foul and fester because of my foolishness; I am utterly bowed down and prostrate; all day long, I go around mourning. For my loins are filled with burning, and there is no soundness in my flesh. I am utterly spent and crushed; I groan because of the tumult of my heart. Psalm 38: 3–8

Hear what other survivors have written:

> The face of someone who has suffered hard pain is different. Though they are smiling and laughing, it is there—a difference. Look around the infusion room—that Something is on every face. The ethnic, gender, age differential makes no difference. The open, vulnerable expectation of a child's face—the smooth, wide-eyed trust is gone on these faces. Pain leaves its mark No makeup, no charade can erase it. There is a depth, a sadness—a latent truth, a hidden wisdom. These souls have taken a dark journey that no well person can share. They have traveled a lonely road as though through fire and overwhelming waters.
>
> The bodies may be rebuilt. The bruises fade in a rainbow of healing colors. The scars scab over. But on the *face* something remains.
>
> We are bonded in a brotherhood of pain and this is our telltale sign—this indescribable imprint that cannot be denied.—Julia, a cancer survivor

Do you recognize a person with cancer now? Have you noticed that you have become more sensitive to others with cancer? The writer, Annie Dillard, who has such a wonderful way with words, described us as "frayed and nibbled survivors." Sharon Carr in her struggle with cancer wrote, "I am weary of being a rag-doll amidst beauty, stitched together because she fell apart."

Those with cancer know the feelings of being ripped and torn and patched together. Cancer has ravaged the body of some. Are we any less precious to God? Can we keep the cheerful hope of a Raggedy Ann doll with our floppy limbs, ganglion legs, bright button eyes and perpetual stitched-on smile, trusting always that we will be held and cherished just as we are by a God who loves us—just as we are. Homey and tattered, our teetering head still smiling brightly, we might even be an emblem.

How do you feel about your body right now? Sometimes it is hard for us to love this new, strange body. Let the mirror of words express your feelings.

I feel that my body is _____

_____

_____

_____

_____

LOSS OF HAIR

Loss of hair is one of the most surprising aspects of many cancers. This dramatically drives home how little control we have in this situation. The loss of hair is a sign of profound transformation. One doctor said the first thing he is asked when someone is diagnosed with cancer is, "Will I lose my hair?" There are many ancient stories and myths that may influence our feelings about the loss of hair. We are reminded of the story of Samson. Is our strength in our hair? Cutting her hair was one of the crimes for which Joan of Arc was condemned. Or perhaps we are reminded of a monk who shaves his head to mark the change from ordinary life to holiness. Or the infant—bald at birth. Many beliefs and traditions surround the cutting of hair. We have been taught that hair is necessary to our beauty. Hair has often been a power statement. And for persons with cancer, it reminds us again how little power and control we have.

> When I lost my hair, my grandchildren called me a bald eagle. Here I am with no hair, no breasts, and wear a sleep mask at night. Now aren't I sexy and classy? With my brain surgery, the scar resembled the letter "S" so I told people that I had my initial tattooed in my head. One Sunday in church our pastor didn't recognize me with my wig on, so I said, "Jim, it's me," and popped the wig off. He said he deserved that and that nothing I did surprised him.—Shelva Mounts

Shelva used humor to cope with her symptoms. In the face of sickness, laughter can sometimes be just the medicine needed.

LIFELINE NO. 11

*Find what is light and funny in you
and record your laughter
to hear again and again
and again and again*

Does humor speed the healing process? On the simplest level a sense of humor can help us focus our attention on something besides ourselves and cancer. On a deeper level it may even mend damaged tissue. Current consensus, according to Oncologist Journal, is that humor has little effect on disease *outcome* but makes a huge impact on the *quality of life* while dealing with cancer.

Humor enables us to see the paradoxes that exist around us. Norman Cousins made a science of laughter as a means of dealing with pain and disease. Locking himself in a hotel room, the story goes, he watched hour after hour of comedy videos and credits this with his eventual cure. In 1979 he wrote about it in *Anatomy of an Illness as Perceived by the Patient.* No one would deny that cancer is very serious but we don't have to always take it so seriously.

As the accumulated struggles of cancer weigh heavy on you, laughter makes things less burdensome. A whole library of cancer jokes has arisen. Google "cancer jokes" and find hundreds of examples.

Write one here that made you laugh. _____

_____

_____

_____

_____

_____

Then laugh out loud if you can. If you can't laugh, smile. Let humor lift your spirits.

Most cancer jokes are dark humor, but this creates a sense of community among cancer patients. Their humor to an outsider may sound cold, but it helps persons deal with the particular stress that cancer presents. Here are a few examples:

Q: What do you call a person who gets numerous occurrences of lymphoma?
A: A lymphomaniac.

Doctor: I've got your test results and some bad news. You have cancer *and* Alzheimer's
Man: Boy, am I lucky. I was afraid I had cancer.

Erma Bombeck, who died of kidney failure due to cancer, left us some wonderful lines:

"Never go to a doctor whose office plants have died."

"Never accept a drink from your urologist."

She also said, "When humor goes, there goes civilization."

DEATH JOKES

Sometimes people with cancer find comfort in joking about death. One researcher found that humorous "death talk" helped people with cancer to think about death without feeling threatened by it.

Some people think laughter helps blood vessels function better because laughter causes the brain to release chemicals that relax muscles and produce pleasure. Some think hearty laughter stimulates the body's immune system and even massages your internal organs. Laughter may not literally cure us, but humor helps us focus on something besides our pain, something beyond ourselves, and promotes a lighter attitude in a heavy situation.

Take a deep breath and try laughing.

Read the story of Sarah in the Bible and how she laughed at the idea of having a baby at her advanced age. (Genesis 21: 6) Now Sarah said, "God has brought laughter for me; everyone who hears will laugh with me." Sometimes humor is the very thing that helps us cope.

DIGNITY

Humor may be a response to the loss of dignity cancer survivors face. Body parts, personal appearance, and bits of our very ego, all of which we have guarded all our lives, are exposed. We are very vulnerable. It is hard to be dignified when you are on the floor, vomiting. Or, as one survivor said, "When my doctor said 'Do not go around crowds because you are susceptible to colds' I thought, 'How could I go anywhere without taking along a couch or toilet?'"

Consider dignity when you are bald from chemo, when you are learning to live with a colostomy, or when you are hooked up to morphine. Obviously coping and getting relief from symptoms is a helpful step in restoring dignity. But dignity is more—it includes maintaining a sense of meaning and purpose and a sense of who you are as an individual. This is difficult when you are losing many things that you normally associate and identify with your sense of personhood.

With cancer our bodies are weak. We see the paradox when people condescend to us or pity us, and so we laugh and remember where our real dignity comes from—in our relationship as a child of God. We affirm that God loves us, frayed and tattered as we may be.

Just as laughter helps you, tears can be a gift in your time of suffering. A good cry can cleanse and refresh you. Tears can restore you. Don't be ashamed to weep with sadness. You may think these actions (laughing and crying) are undignified. Not so. Society at large has an extremely narrow definition of dignity. It is no small thing to have your body rearranged.

One of the most inspiring moments is to see someone you have known or seen who has maintained a sense of dignity during a cancer ordeal. Recall and name that person. Reflect on his/her characteristics. What do you think enabled that person to keep a sense of dignity? How did he/she exemplify it? Jackie wrote:

> I learned so much from Charles during my treatment. Even though he had full body radiation, the results would be in the future. He would develop leukemia. His decision for the treatment gave him seven years to be with his family and also enjoy his motorcycle. He was a great friend that gave so many cancer survivors hope and taught us how to make each day special. He was quiet, and we drew strength from his dignity.

Charles seemed to have been able to express things that spoke to the essence of who he was. The fact that he could speak freely of things that made his life worthwhile in spite of all his challenges and losses resulted in his sense of peace and dignity.

As a cancer survivor, examine your own sense of dignity by thinking about your life, particularly those parts that you think are most important. What do you feel most proud of?

Humans have the right to be treated with dignity regardless of the level of dependency or need. Even a hopeless struggle can have meaning and dignity. Although we can't always affect how others treat us, we can conduct ourselves in a dignified manner. Being treated with dignity begins with our own self-respect, acceptance, and self-honoring. Sometimes very simple things can improve our attitude. One survivor suggested that dignity can be expressed by keeping yourself as clean as possible.

Innovative workshops which focus on ways to help persons undergoing cancer treatment enhance their appearance and feel better about themselves are being presented at some cancer centers. Wigs are provided and scarves and colorful turbans. Some survivors chose new, shorter hair styles, and some shave their heads as treatments begin. Through their bald period, some cancer patients boldly show their spunk by wearing baseball hats announcing their favorite team. Some cosmetic firms give free makeup kits and demonstrations on how to use them. Soothing beauty rituals, fragrant lotions and powders, all help you love your body in small ways. Be especially kind to yourself at this time. Self compassion instills a sense of calm and inner strength.

Sometimes it helps to meditate on your scars and bruises. You can thank the body for its continuous battle toward wellness as it tries so hard to repair itself. Your body, a faithful companion, works through great difficulties with an amazing tenacity. The life force is strong. Thank the veins in your arms and hands for their endurance. Appreciate the beauty of bruises in their rainbow of colors and shapes. Thank the scars that make broken places stronger. Respect the body's own rhythm of timing and healing.

A LOOK AT SIDE EFFECTS

Isn't it enough that we go through all these bodily changes? Do we have to have all these side effects *too*?

Aa a part of accepting your new body image, let's look at a list of those repulsive symptoms you live with. There are a series of mundane discomforts, one after another, that many cancer survivors experience, especially with chemotherapy. It's time to talk of:

Fatigue

Nausea

Weight loss

Diarrhea

Constipation

Hair Loss

Tingling in feet and toes

Muddled thinking

Body itches

Mouth sores

Shaking in different degrees of intensity

Mental confusion

Collapsed veins

What the body is able to endure is almost unbelievable.

"What is my body doing?" you may wonder. It is hard to realize these symptoms are letting us know things about ourselves in the only way our body can talk to us. Your body knows something awful is being done to it. Though medical advances continue to improve in ways to counter the side effects, it is no small thing the body is going through. You are reminded through cancer that you need to revive and strengthen your inner values to get through this.

From a world where you made lists and set goals, you are plunged into a maelstrom of surprising symptoms and changing agendas. Time and again we keep learning: We are not in control. You feel as if you are caught in a whirlpool. There is a story from the ancient Greeks of the hero, Odysseus. He and his men were sailing by a treacherous whirlpool, using all their skills and courage to keep from being sucked into this maelstrom. They personified this whirlpool and gave it a name: Charybdis.

Can this method of imaging and naming work for you? When you name something, in a small way you do control it or at least are able to endure it. You defang the tiger. The fearful experience becomes a bearable sojourn. Give the side effects you are going through a name that amuses you, or creates a pleasant image, or is so horrible and exaggerated it surpasses credibility. Absurdity and silliness are permitted.

The experience of enduring seemingly unending chemo sessions might be called "Plodding through Purgatory." Images may arise of Frodo, the Hobbit, doggedly keeping on through rings of fire; or the journey of Orpeheus into the Underworld, past the many-headed hound, Cerberus. Just the image of "Keep on Keeping On," or those bumper stickers you see on large trucks, "Keep on Trucking," may bring a smile to your face.

LIFELINE NO. 25

There are smiles and light within you. Reach deep and let them out

---

Name the days when you are experiencing bad side effects. You may have "Catatonic Days" when all you can do is sit and stare. Remember the scene from a Harry Potter movie where, with a wave of the wand and the uttering of *Petrificus Totalus*, a person was put into a temporary, paralyzed state.

Some days you may name "Eggshell Days" when you feel so fragile you think you will crack. Afraid to move or be touched, you want to be very still/very inward. You try to just hold yourself together if you can.

There are "Mule-Kicking Days" when your insides feel as if they have undergone a losing bout with a kicking mule.

And always, surprisingly, there are "Rainbow Days," when you feel good, when unexpected respite comes and you have the visceral feeling of a deep surge in the body toward wellness. On those days the world is full of color.

On days when you are first infused with chemicals, you feel as if your whole body has been zapped. To borrow a word from a Superman or Captain Marvel comic, you experience a "Kryptonite day."

Maybe you have known your personal hoof-and-mouth disease which you might call "Cardboard Mouth" day. It is as if a layer of cardboard coats the roof of your mouth and permeates all you taste.

"Bad Hair" days are common as handfuls of hair fall out.

"Call the Plumber" days abound.

"Rag Doll Weakness" days are frequent.

Our culture values mastery and control. We tip our hats to self-sufficiency and independence. But the truth for us cancer patients is that we have needs and discomforts and suffering.

Bring your imagination into play and claim for yourself the power of naming.

As well as naming your side effects, you may want to record and track them. Symptoms and how severe they are vary from person to person and day to day. As you record them, patterns may appear. You can track your "good days' and your "not so good" days. Again this gives you a feeling of control. Sometimes all we can do is just breathe gently through the difficult side-effects and lean on God's strength.

In a cancer world, where we can be far too preoccupied with the ugly nature of things, art can help us see something beautiful to overcome the darkness.

COLOR A MANDALA

A mandala is a geometric pattern within a circular framework on which to meditate. It is an ancient art form that developed independently in many parts of the world. Mandalas are found in Asian, Celtic, Egyptian, European, Indian, Islamic and Native American cultures. It is a soul-satisfying combination of geometry and color. It is not for a specific treatment of any disability or pain, but rather for the enhancement of general well-being. Using crayons or fine pointed markers, fill in the geometric forms in the coloring book. Choose colors that are beautiful and that speak to you.

There are a number of mandala coloring books on the market. It can be satisfying for someone with cancer to take the chaos of colors and put them in a structured form. Just as we come into the world hardwired to hear noise and make a language out of it, in the same way, we find satisfaction in taking a myriad of colors and imposing structure on them.

If you like to create random patterns with a compass and ruler, or if you like to just fool around with geometric doodles, you might like to create your own mandalas.

All mandalas begin with a circle symbolizing the endless circle of life with no beginning and no end, the entire universe. Within the circle you can create triangles and squares or any other basic geometric form (a hexagon or rhombus, octagon, etc.), which symbolizes your containment within the entire universe.

Create a still center point in your mandala from which the other shapes radiate. You may create other circles, arcs and lines all radiating out of the center. Strive for precision, proportion, and balance, and a design that is pleasing to you.

You might want to include nature shapes within your mandala, such as a leaf or flower or vine. Contemplating nature shapes has a calming effect on the senses and the soul. Study your design and then just gaze quietly at it.

Meditating on your mandala quietens your mind. Insight comes to the surface and your perceptions are enhanced. Just absorb the image without trying to analyze it. Our learning here is intuitive rather than intellectual. As you color these universal patterns of line and form, you shift from the distractions of a cancer world to a place of simplicity and peace. Tensions are alleviated and serenity enhanced. It can open your mind to a greater understanding of God and your place in the cosmos.

CHAPTER 6
Blessings with Cancer

We come to the end of your workbook. We have been concentrating in this book on a key moment in your life—a real turning point—a single incident, really—your challenge with cancer. This is an important event to consider because it is a crisis moment—a time where both danger and opportunity come together. You have begun looking at the fears, dreams, feelings, experiences, and thoughts cancer has brought you, trying to gain some self-understanding through this experience, some reorganization of your life and your thinking now that you are a cancer survivor. You were given dark nights. If not treated as growth, they will destroy you.

Hopefully, you won't stop seeking to learn about yourself through every stage of your cancer. Let this be just the beginning for you. This workbook is a self portrait of where you are now. It is a story that is still evolving. It is like asking the old farmer: "Have you lived here all your life?" and he says "Not yet."

Consider now: What have you lost with cancer? What have you gained? What did it take from you and what has it given you? Listen to some of these survivors. You may be surprised to discover that the gains most often outweighed the losses because, like the Velveteen Rabbit in the children's storybook, you become more real through this experience. Sickness is a force that brings growth and seasoned understanding and can lead to a new depth of happiness.

"When I think of what cancer took from me I come up with a very short list: 1. A non-essential body part (a breast). I like what the journalist Linda Ellerbe said: 'Hey it's not like it's a *foot*—It is just a breast.' 2. A few rather tough weeks out of my life.

"The things cancer gave me make a longer list: 1. A greater awareness of time—the importance of each day. 2. A greater appreciation of family and friends. 3. Incentive to fulfill goals and finish unfinished projects. 4. A new sense of my own strength. 5. A closer relationship with God and a deeper faith."—Pat, a cancer survivor

"Cancer has changed my life in many ways. I am stronger and I have a much deeper faith. It has helped me to re-gain my self-confidence, but most importantly I've faced my mortality and learned to live my life to the fullest. I believe that God put me to this test so I would look over my life and finish living it with hope, joy, and a surety that is pleasing to him alone. Cancer could have taken a lot from me, but I turned this negative into positives. It took insecurity and changed it to belief in my self-worth; it took self-doubt and changed it into self-confidence, and it took the rest of my doubts and changed them into a fighting spirit and self-respect. Cancer has empowered me to be myself, who I really am, waking me up to an active and purposeful life. A Scripture I relate to is from Romans 5:3–4. 'We also rejoice in our sufferings because we know that suffering produces perseverance, perseverance character, and character, hope.'"—Fay, a cancer survivor

"Since I'm six years out, cancer is no longer the first thing I think of when I wake, or the last thing I think of before sleeping. I do think that somewhere inside, I have the fear that it may come back and get me one day. I think that's a fear many survivors carry around with them. I attended a breast cancer support group for a while and I've seen some dear friends lose their fight with cancer.

I have so much admiration for the way these women lived the last days of their lives, not in fear, but with grace and dignity, even though they knew their gallant fight would not prevail. I feel so blessed to have known these strong, brave women. I think having had cancer has taken away my naiveté that bad things would never happen in my life. On the other hand, it's made me appreciate the value of my family and good friends. It's made me think twice before feeling sorry for myself and I don't 'sweat the small stuff' so much any more. The words of a children's song says it best for me: 'I thank the Lord for giving me the things I need, the sun, the rain and the apple trees. The Lord's been good to me!'"— Barbara Haga, a cancer survivor

In stories like these we discover our most profound lessons. These narratives and many others like them illustrate how pain and isolation become transformed into gratitude and renewed communion with loved ones and God. We look back over our trials and recognize that we have been visited by grace.

LIFELINE NO. 43
You can never really run out of visions of hope

Were any of these survivors' stories similar to yours? Where would you agree or disagree?

Time and again in this workbook, we have dealt with the loss of control that cancer brings to our lives. All of us want to believe that we are in charge, that by will and determination our ego will not only survive, but conquer. But in order to maintain control we must have answers. In cancer, there are no simple answers. We come to understand that suffering is beyond us. Healing is, too. Sooner or later we must give all of this up. Let go and put everything in God's hands. The Twelve Step program for Alcoholics Anonymous acknowledges "my life is unmanageable." This speaks to us, also. It requires a trust in a larger pattern that the mind does not understand and a willingness to go on without understanding.

We may discover with cancer that our faith, which we thought until now was strong, is indeed weak, and that our trust in God was shallow. Cancer demands more of us than mouthings of faith. None of us really knows how we would act in a challenging situation until we have been through it. Cancer gives us this opportunity to learn how strong our faith really is. We learn to let go of a faith that is effort and will on our part and turn to a faith that is surrender. We discover that grace is a gift; a gift available to all. Gratitude becomes our response. Gratitude eventually converts the pangs of memory into a tranquil joy. We learn to affirm the redemptive value of suffering; how being wounded brings about healing.

Listen to another survivor's testimony that the darkness of sickness can never obscure the light of the gracious gifts we have been given.

> "My ultimate lesson in cancer did not come from my 11 years as an oncology social worker and coordinator and facilitator of the Cancer Support Group programs. My life's lesson came in 1980 when the whirlwind and excitement from college acceptance and a basketball scholarship were completely extinguished, and replaced by extreme fear, incredible shock, and profound disbelief when I was diagnosed with a rare form of bone cancer at the ripe old age of 17. Time simply seemed to stand still—surreal. Everybody around me—my mom, my dad, my family, my friends—all seemed to be frozen into their own separate vacuum. We weren't very functional back then, but who could be in this circumstance? Anyway, my life changed at that moment. My innocence was lost and growing up didn't seem so exciting anymore. Turning 18 through all of this seemed such a paradox. I could buy beer. I could go to R-rated movies. I could vote for the President.

Instead, I had to put my signature on a line at the bottom of a yellow consent form giving permission for my right leg to be amputated at the mid-thigh. The Senior Prom "No Drinking" contract was where my signature was supposed to have been written.

"The very good news came after a very lonely 12 hours, the eve of my surgery, wondering what would it be like to have one leg, and if my family and friends would still love me if I were different. Dr. Enneding saved my leg after a five-hour surgery. He pioneered the limb-salvaging technique. Pain and challenges now took on a whole new meaning. I can't even begin to describe the pain I experienced from that surgery. And again another paradox, thank God I had a leg. But it hurt beyond words. This was long before the days of the PCA pumps. I had to wait out every minute of those 4 hours until the next shot. My next several months were spent in physical therapy, in great pain, learning to maneuver on crutches, living in my new home and with my new family—the Howard Johnson's Gang of Gainesville, Florida—and radiation therapy treatments on a twice a day schedule. I was totally consumed within my thoughts about "what in the world had happened to me?" I was just plain quiet. Thinking too much landed me in a very dark and scary place. So I slept and slept and slept. I lived to sleep. Sleeping kept me from thinking. My friends back in Virginia were planning our senior class trip, graduation, and parties. I lived to sleep. Our worlds were far apart—and my next 15 months were spent on crutches.

"It has been 22 years since those difficult moments. There are many, many more complicated facets to this story. I have chosen to share only a glimpse of its beginning. I got cancer. I was young. My life changed. I had to move away. Normal will never be what it was. People acted weird around me. My family didn't talk. I was angry. Yet, I survived! Hope is a great thing!

"I am 40 years old now. I am happily married and have a beautiful five-year-old son. There are times when this part of my life seems like a recurring bad dream. And then there are times I just shake my head in utter amazement that this painful, angry period in my life didn't land me in a destructive lifestyle. I've learned that what felt to me at the time as lost innocence wasn't really lost at all. It was divinely preserved and is what guides me today with strength, wisdom, empathy, and love."—Robin Yoder, Director, Hawthorne Cancer Center, Richmond, Virginia

We have not talked about prayer and the place of prayer in healing, but throughout this workbook you *have* been praying. There are many ways to pray. You pray by walking, by writing, by observing, by asking questions, through art, and through music. All these methods are a chance to walk with God through the great challenges you face. Though we can attest to the healing power of prayer, prayer is a spiritual expression that enables us to remember that this cancer occurrence has more to do with spiritual healing than strengthening the immune system.

Questions arise such as, "Why me? What is death? How can this feel like a blessing?" There may be no answers, but we find serenity in asking and the questions deepen. We affirm the ultimate; the highest we can know is that we do not know. All of our suffering—all of our life—is ultimately a mystery. But we do know that God is with us with each small step we take. Faith is surrendering to this mystery and believing that an unconditional love is the underpinning of it all. Go into the heart of prayer, and pray that you may be strengthened with wisdom and insight. Meditate on Isaiah 43:1&2:

> But now thus says the LORD, he who created you, O Jacob, he who formed you, O Israel: Do not fear, for I have redeemed you; I have called you by name, you are mine. When you pass through the waters, I will be with you; and through the rivers, they shall not overwhelm you; when you walk through fire you shall not be burned, and the flame shall not consume you.

Let's review what we have been doing together these past six chapters and see if any patterns have emerged that will help you in understanding yourself. In Chapter 1, you looked first at your uniqueness—getting the big picture of your whole life that brought you to this moment. Then you sought to recall a happy childhood memory. There were two reasons for doing this. First, just to get you in the habit of recalling, and second, to remind you of those happy memories you have somewhere in your life. These positive moments can help in your healing process. You are using memory to put balance back in your life so that your life is more than this one cancer moment. Our learning points were these:

1. You are much more than your cancer, and

2. All of us have happy memories to access.

In Chapter 2, emphasis was on the importance of deliberately choosing what you see, making the point that in spite of cancer, life can still be a celebration. You sought especially to be open to surprises—not to expect things to happen in any particular way. Our learning points were:

1. What makes the difference is not the event, but the eyes through which it is seen, and

2. What you see is what you get, but what you choose to see says a lot about who you are.

Your individual cancer story was the main point of Chapter 3. Your story needs to be told over and over—especially sharing with those who have also experienced cancer. How do you tell it? You recalled the impact of hearing your cancer diagnosis and looked by your response to this news, at who you were at the moment of impact and how it affects who you are now. You can learn about yourself from your response to this event. You looked at your cancer story from different angles: interviews with your doctor—telling your family. You also looked at other ways to respond to this news. Learning points were:

1. Fear and anxiety are a natural response to a cancer diagnosis, and

2. You determine how you cope with the news that cancer has entered your life.

In Chapter 4 you dealt with your treatments and pain and considered your individual level of patience, endurance, and courage. Learning points:

1. Patience develops as we move from "I" to "Eye,"

2. Cancer is what it is, and as such, takes its place in our own cycle of life, and

3. In the midst of it all, God is with us.

In Chapter 5, we considered body changes and image. You reflected on ways of coping with symptoms and side effects. Learning points:

1. Humor, tears, and acceptance of our new body image helps in the healing, and

2. Naming puts us in charge of our symptoms.

Finally, in Chapter 6 you looked at your wholeness and considered what you have lost and what you have gained as a cancer survivor.

It is the unique challenge of each person who faces sickness to discover their personal way to cope. By studying aspects of yourself, after a while you can discern patterns and begin to see what your journey with cancer is all about. Flip back through this workbook and look for recurring images or words or themes in your replies to questions or in some statement that caught your attention. Patterns are there. Sometimes they are like photography slides that are out of order. Sometimes this self understanding jumps out at you quickly, but often it is years later that you see the story clearly. How you choose to respond begins to form a pattern. Look for ways you engage or hold back in life. What is it about on the surface? What is it *really* about? Uncover your "ah has." You are weaving the tapestry of your world every day, and you need to know what design you are making.

Fay said:

> "I named my workbook 'Humpty Dumpty' because it describes so well my new life. The inspiring thought I had is from the child's nursery rhyme. Humpty-Dumpty sat on a wall. Humpty

Dumpty had a great fall. But that was not to be the end. For God put me back together again."

With cancer, you see how parts of yourself make you whole and what connections have tied your life together. How would you sum up in a sentence or phrase a simple way of coping that has been useful to you and that you could recommend to other survivors? What helped you get through it? Or what helps you now in the midst of it?

Here are the responses of some cancer survivors:

Shelva—humor

Fay—faith

Jackie—hope

Gloria—altruism (helping somebody else)

Lea—support of friends

Robin—sleep

Jane—music

Elaine—mantra "Yahweh"

Pat—support of family

It's time to consider how far you have already come as a cancer survivor—to take stock of your coping, whether your cancer journey has just recently begun or whether you are a long-term survivor.

Whenever our lives are probed deeply, a metaphor appears. Consider the metaphor of a mountain. Picture in your mind some great, spectacular mountain, majestic and reaching to the heavens. Perhaps a mountain in the Rockies or the Himalayas or a high peak in your area. Stay with this image until you feel a sense of awe at the scale of such beauty. Next, consider the challenge of climbing such a mountain.

Now, as you trudge on toward the peak, ask yourself: "What do I expect to enjoy at the top? And if you looked down from the height of this mountain what might you see about your life? What insight does this vista give you?" Write your answer here:

_____

_____

_____

_____

_____

To reinforce this imagery, find a small, round, water-smoothed stone to carry in your pocket. Let it be for you a praying stone. Finger its size and texture. Let it serve as a grounding in your life or as a symbol of how much you have endured, how far you have come. Let it remind you that "God is my rock and my salvation." When anxiety is high and hope is low, finger this stone and find strength and calmness.

Cancer is a stripping away, a leaving bare. As a chicken breaking out of a shell, we are exposed and vulnerable. Cancer may even be an extreme ravishment for some—the sacred house of the body completely plundered, the body stripped of its flesh, the soul laid bare.

LIFELINE NO. 14
We can heal ourselves over and over again

The experience of survivorship is a broadening of consciousness and sensitivity. Cancer has forced us to face a greater pain than even our physical ailments. We are forced to resolve for ourselves the issues of life and death. Death cannot be ignored. And because of that, we discover poignancy, an aliveness, a vitality as we face up to our mortality.

Death is a challenging, perplexing subject in all cultures. Sometimes other traditions help us see our situation more clearly. Consider the Tibetan Traditions of Death.

1. All die. Nothing can be done to turn it away.
2. Our time is continually running out on us in an unbroken stream. The clock is ticking.
3. We find very little time to dedicate to spiritual practice. Before we are ready, death is upon us.

Cancer forces us to face these truths. Death, for some, is the greatest of all fears, the terror of the unknown.

Look at Tradition 1. In cancer, we realize how much of our lives have been spent avoiding this truth, guarding against facing it. "Death is something that happens, but not to us," we think. How frantically we have run from facing it, surrounding ourselves with all manner of distractions. Reflecting on this statement can take us into solitude where beauty and mystery are illuminated. Do we run from being alone because we fear death? Only by facing death can we develop real passion for being alive. Cancer teaches you that you are never more alive than when you are looking death in the face.

Consider Tradition 2. Cancer survivors realize in contemplating this statement that we have been blessed with time not only to contemplate our demise but also to attend to unfinished business. We are filled with a new sense of urgency. With the clock ticking we must now do those things and say those words we have always meant to say and do sometime in the future. Write an open letter to a person in your life sharing something you want to say, an "I never told you" letter. Then, write some thank-you notes of gratitude to persons who touched your life and you never thanked.

As we contemplate Tradition 3, we realize there is no time left for superficial spirituality. We turn to finding more meaningful ways of living our final days. Cancer forces us to focus like a laser on what is important. There is no time for greed, avarice, selfishness, competitiveness, or pride. There is only time to let go—to rest in the Divine. Death, the utterly personal meeting with the unimaginable, happens not at some convenient ending place in our lives but right in the middle. There is only time to see life as it really is—so precious!—so lovely!— and to stand on the edge of the abyss and fall into the unknown, confident that the God of unconditional love will be there to catch us. We affirm that no matter how grave the future, grace triumphs in the end.

Our focus for this study has been more about renewal than recovery. We will never "be well' in the same sense again. But we may be better. Life, after a critical illness, does not go back to where it was before. This unwanted experience has made us richer and surer.

This ordeal of a survivor becomes an experience of growth and self-realization. After experiencing cancer, you may have a new understanding of what constitutes happiness, and your ideas of what is essential may shift. Cancer can highlight the emptiness or inadequacy of the way you normally live, and give you at least a glimpse of how life can be.

SECTION II

Leader's Guide

Introduction to Leader's Guide

Why have our churches been slow to respond to the concerns of cancer survivors? There may be many reasons. First there seems to be a mind-set that cancer is a medical problem, "Let the medical community deal with this one." Medical care is certainly needed, but cancer survivors also need assistance in dealing with the psycho-spiritual traumas produced by a diagnosis of cancer. Every physical or medical trauma inflicted upon a person will always produce some kind of spiritual trauma. It in no way competes with medical and psychological physicians, but in a manner supplementary to, and complementary of, each can help a stronger, truly "healthy" individual emerge.

A practical factor in our local churches is the problem of prioritizing. When overworked church leaders, especially those without a support staff, have to distribute their time and commitments to many good causes, cancer survivors may be overlooked and neglected. "We can't do everything!" one pastor said. In addition, church leaders may feel they do not have the expertise or first hand experience to deal with such a group. Where is there a seminary class offering church leaders guidance in this area? Developing a group for cancer survivors is not among the traditional ministries for which a pastor has received training.

Finally, our faith communities seem to see the scattering of cancer survivors as unique; for example: one teen with bone cancer, one 50-year-old woman with breast cancer, one 70-year-old man with kidney cancer, and on and on. We tend to see in units of one, and for the most part these members of our congregation must bear their burden alone. Leader and congregants tend not to think in terms of the *group* of suffering persons. Although we have Sunday school classes for multiple age groups, and offer Lenten Studies for multiple interest groups, and though we arrange for differently-gifted people to go on diverse kinds of service ministries, we often fail to offer helping groups for that significant number of persons in our churches who have been forced to face this life-threatening disease and all the bruises this causes on the human spirit.

Our mission is to help these friends and colleagues reassess their faith; enlarge their understanding of the Grace of God; work through their anger and disappointment; and seek resolution of their doubts and affirmation for whatever number of days may still be in their future. What a wonderful opportunity we have in the church to help cancer survivors turn a turbulent, awful illness into a spiritual pilgrimage toward a fulfilling life!

You are ready to begin a class for cancer survivors who are seeking to learn from this experience. Where and how do you begin? What I offer here are only suggestions, based on my experiences leading such groups. Take the ideas that are helpful to you and discard the others. I begin with the assumption that there is not an existing cancer group in your church, though you are probably aware of several persons who are cancer survivors. Make a list of these persons. Your pastor, or perhaps a prayer group in your church, may have names for you. With as few as four names, you are ready to begin.

This class is structured to be used over a six-week period, such as Lent. Lent seems an appropriate time to begin since it symbolizes our spiritual journey to Easter. The significance of this is that the mordant despair of Ash Wednesday is a necessary prelude to the triumphant spirit of Easter. In the same way, the agony and sadness of cancer are a necessary prelude to self-realization. However, cancer does not occur in seasons, so feel free to begin whenever it suits your schedule and situation. Nor do you have to conform to six weeks. Stretch or condense the sessions as it is appropriate for you and the group. I do suggest, however, that you have an ending date in mind when you begin.

One and a half hours seems to be a good time frame for each session. You may prefer a longer period of time with a break between; however, the difficulty I found with this was that the sessions create a certain mood and encourage discussion in a particular direction, and it was hard to get the group back together after a break. Another factor in favor of one and a half hour session is the endurance limitations of some participants, who may be under medication or experiencing that bone-tired fatigue chemo brings.

WHO IS THIS CLASS FOR?

Only cancer survivors. Caregivers often want to come along or even need to come along for transportation help, but I *strongly suggest* that they do not come into the classroom. I allowed a caregiver to come to one of my classes. At one point in the first session, when participants were recalling a happy childhood memory, she leaned over and read her husband's (the cancer survivor) entry and said, "You never told me that." Although a harmless statement in itself, it produced an awkward moment for the class and broke down the bonding between members. She herself felt uncomfortable about whether or not to join in the conversations or just sit quietly. One Christian educator suggested to me that it might solve the problem by having a class for caregivers running simultaneously.

After deciding who is *not* to come to the class, who *does* come? A cancer survivor at any stage of their cancer. I had a person who had just received her diagnosis in the same class with a 30-year-survivor, and that worked well. I had one member who was confined to her bed but she "attended" the class by email and was a helpful addition. The class is for both men and women, and there is no age restriction. I personally have not had a child in my class, however. The class is not for any one particular type of cancer. There are enough similarities in cancer experiences to be helpful to all survivors.

Now, with names in hand and a place and date and time to begin, how do we get participants to come? This turned out to be not as easy as I thought it might. There is something about cancer that is off-putting. It is such a personal subject, and persons may feel that they will be put on the spot and embarrassed in some way. We discovered that a personal invitation works well. Here is a sample of one that I sent, just a simple computer-generated invitation.

> This is a special invitation to you to attend a class with a select
> group of persons who have been told, "You have cancer."
> Just as Lent is a six-week period in the Church Year when we

contemplate Jesus' journey to Jerusalem, we, too, will meet for six weeks to look at our unique journey with cancer. We will share our stories in order to examine, understand, and reflect on how our story fits in with God's story.

We invite you to join this group, which will meet on (day) at (time) for one to one and a half hours beginning (calendar date).

If you are unable to attend we invite you to join our class by email.

With an approximate number, I was ready to begin. The class works best with not more than twelve participants. In each church where I lead a class, we also put announcements in the church bulletin and newsletter. In both situations, persons came to the class who had not received a personal invitation and were cancer survivors that the congregation did not know about.

Another difficulty in beginning is that this is a brand new type of ministry. Participants may have had experiences with other cancer support groups. There are groups that are just for fellowship and there are those that are just opportunities for a member to unload and unleash all their feelings. A person with previous experience in another type of cancer group may bring a different agenda to the meeting.

The purpose of this study is for cancer survivors to seek to learn about themselves in this particular situation.

I recommend that if possible the class be taught by a cancer survivor, but this is not essential. A good class facilitator works just as well.

Session 1 Guide

PREPARATION

1. Before the first session, ask each participant to bring to the first meeting a picture of himself or herself as a child.
2. Ensure that each participant has a copy of *Fear Not! Learning From Your Cancer.*
3. Gather all the supplies you will need for this session.
4. Prepare nametags if you decide to use them. If you don't use nametags, it is helpful to have a place card with first names on the table in front of each participant, especially for the first meeting.
5. Arrange the meeting room as invitingly as you can. If possible, seat the participants around a table in a horseshoe shape so that participants can see one another. You will need a blackboard or newsprint or PowerPoint on which to draw as you explain the Oak of Righteousness. You may choose to use a CD player and CD for part of the session.

Supplies: colored markers or crayons; extra notebook paper and pencils for those who might need them, Bibles.

WELCOME TO THE FIRST SESSION

Welcome the participants as they arrive. Discuss how they learned about the class. Be sure to get names, addresses, and Email addresses. When all are assembled, go around the circle having each participant give his/her name, their type of cancer, and its stage of development.

GOALS FOR THIS SESSION

- Create a comfortable setting where participants will feel free to interact and begin bonding with other survivors
- Help participants begin to see the whole pattern of their lives, the distinctiveness that defines and affirms each.
- Give survivors a wider view of their individual lives than the all-consuming moment with cancer.
- Help participants accent the happy childhood memories that can serve as a strong foundation as they journey through cancer.

SOME CHALLENGES YOU MAY ENCOUNTER THIS SESSION

It is important as you begin the introductions to stress that you want *only* the name, the type of cancer, and the stage. Emphasize that there will be time as the class continues to tell more of their cancer story. Some survivors may be intrigued with their own story and tend to go on and on. In consideration of others, it is necessary to structure this first response. If you are a cancer survivor yourself, you can model the response you want by beginning the sharing. Simply state your name, your cancer, the stage you are in currently. Most members of the class will know that in Stage 1, the tumor is small and localized. By stage 4, it has spread invasively to other organs and nodes. Some members of the class will be in remission.

SESSION PLAN

Oaks of Righteousness

Read the Scripture passage.

> The Spirit of the Lord is upon me
> To comfort all who mourn and provide for those who mourn in
> Zion.

To give them a garland instead of ashes,
The oil of gladness instead of mourning,
The mantle of praise instead of a faint spirit.
They will be called Oaks of Righteousness, the planting of the
    LORD
to display his splendor. Isaiah 61:2b-4

Explain that each student will draw his/her own Oak of Righteousness on p. 25. Have art paper available for those participants who may not yet have the workbook. Give the students all the time they need to draw and ponder the various steps of this art project.

I have found this to be a good beginning activity for the class. The artwork is not too challenging and the participants relax. There may be bantering back and forth as they work. In one class I remember a participant saying playfully, "Now don't rush me. I want plenty of time to complete my achievement fruits."

Close this portion of the class by emphasizing the uniqueness of each person, using the words in the workbook if you like, or creating your own. Stress the learning point:

You are more than your Cancer. It is only one part of who you are.

Gather up the supplies you used for the drawing of the tree. Participants may take their drawings home with them and continue to ponder and supplement their discoveries.

Childhood Pictures

For the second portion of the session, ask the participants to get out the childhood picture each was asked to bring. Pass these around the class. Participants may want to remark informally on the pictures.

Invite the class to get in a comfortable position, then lower the lights. Ask them to close their eyes. Lead them in the breathing exercise on p. 26 of recalling themselves as children. This type of meditation, which will be used throughout these sessions, may be new to the group.

At first students may not be able to keep their minds on their breathing. A waterfall of thoughts may interfere. Students may need to stay with this practice many times before they go to the second part, where they try on the in-breath to recall themselves as young children.

When they have opened their eyes and lights are turned back on, tell the class that they will each share a happy childhood memory.

Someone may ask, "What if I had an unhappy childhood—what then?" I have never had anyone in any of my classes who could not recall a simple, happy, childhood memory. I believe the basic values of love and compassion are present in us from the time of our birth and that young children have that wonderful gift of finding pleasure anywhere. Look at the pictures we see on TV of young children playing in the rubble of war. The participants in the class are asked to go back to that trusting, innocent child in themselves, who saw each day as a wonderful, new adventure.

Read the samples of childhood memories of survivors included in the workbook on pp. 27-28. Then ask each participant to recall his/her own childhood pleasure. If class members are willing to do so, have them write a paragraph recalling this experience. If they do not want to write, have them just remember and then jot down a few words that bring the memory back. Emphasize that you are seeking the memory of some simple pleasure each knew as a child. Use the jump start suggestions in the workbook on p. 26, if needed. The survivor is not just indulging in nostalgia, but is gleaning from the past that which affirms his/her basic joy in living.

Allow at least 15 minutes for this pondering and remembering. You may want to play soft music as they recall and reflect. As the leader, a bonus to this activity is that you can watch the class members' faces soften and glow as they remember these happy experiences.

Ask those who are willing to read their memory to the rest of the class. This is another excellent bonding activity.

HOMEWORK FOR NEXT SESSION

As the class prepares to leave, give them an assignment. Invite them to look each day for something that surprises them and something that inspires them.

In addition, ask them to observe a child this week; to take a moment and just stare at a child. Stare in that absorbed way that children often stare, accepting everything just as it is, always in the present moment. If possible choose a happy child with no particular agenda. Invite them to feel the spirit of the child. See the essence of that child.

Session 2 Guide

PREPARATION

These first two sessions seek to affirm a survivor's self-worth. They are a pause wherein survivors consider who they were before cancer, who they are during the ordeal of cancer, and who they will become after taking this cancer journey.

Supplies: Pictures of a seashell and an artichoke, or actual objects to contemplate; Bibles

WHAT WE LEARNED LAST SESSION

It is hoped that this session will build on the previous one. Where we stressed the uniqueness of our lives and the happy memories of our childhood in the former session, this session stresses that all happy memories are not in the past, but are available to us in the here and now.

By way of review, you might remind the class members that we are seeking to clarify our experience with cancer and see what we can learn about ourselves through this process. We have learned that you have happy memories that you can build on that can affirm your basic worth. You may say, "No matter how much of your past is no longer available, there are always additional memories to retrieve. You lived through those happy times and you need to claim them." Now we add to this foundation the notion that all good memories are not in the past. Jewell, by email, wrote to the class, "Much of our joy is like the unexpected lighting of a butterfly on your shoulder. Enjoy the moment, for the magic will soon be gone, but while it is with you, it is a true gift from heaven."

GOALS FOR THIS SESSION

The purpose of this session is to continue to build a foundation for our dealing with our cancer experience. It is an upbeat session. It can also be an "ah-ha" session for some survivors as they pinpoint where it is that they find inspiration, and realize that this is a place they can return to again and again. It can also broaden their outlook as they hear where others find inspiration. One member enlightened us all as she explained how she listens to the nightly news, which most often seems to contain bad news, but she finds inspiration and awareness of ways she and others can still be of service.

In Thornton Wilder's play, *Our Town*, Emily has died but is granted one day to return to the life she has lived. She looks at the preciousness of ordinary events. She sees her Mother preparing breakfast as usual and Emily cries out, "Look at me!" This is the purpose of this week's assignment. Encourage the class to look around. *Really look* to see that they are surrounded by surprises and inspiration.

Sometimes when we are first diagnosed with cancer, things in the world around us take on new value. Common, everyday things become awesome. As our years in remission grow, things may become dulled, commonplace again. One of the things cancer does is wake us up, startle us, open our eyes to blessings we may have taken for granted. We are reminded of the words of Robert Louis Stevenson: "The world is so full of a number of things. I'm sure we should all be happy as kings!"

SOME CHALLENGES YOU MAY ENCOUNTER THIS SESSION

Sometimes this awareness can be too intense. As the miracle of Spring's arrival awakened many in our class, one woman was overwhelmed. Her daughter had died just before she herself received her diagnosis of cancer and she felt that she could not welcome Spring this year. She could not even bear to go outdoors in the midst of sunshine and beauty. She was, at that moment, in a very dark place, and she needed this time of hibernating for her soul to find peace in solitude. The fact that she even came to the class at all showed her resilience.

The second week also proved too much for another member of one of my classes. He came to me after attending the first session and said the class was too difficult for him; the other survivors were getting better, were getting back in a more normal flow of life; he was getting worse. I was sorry that he dropped out, but I realized we must each listen to what our mind and body tells us. I also came to realize that being introspective about our cancer experience can sometimes be harder for men than for women. Some men have not been taught to deal with vulnerability; they tend to deny the inner fears and weaknesses cancer always brings. Yet cancer can melt this "macho" image.

SESSION PLAN

If there are newcomers to the class, welcome them and have them introduce themselves in the same manner as participants did last week. If anyone is absent, report on him/her, if this information is known. (I found in almost all of my sessions that someone had a doctor's appointment or just did not feel up to attending that day.) If a participant was having a serious problem with a cancer symptom, we began our session by naming that person, followed with a moment of silent prayer while we held that person before God in our thoughts, with love.

Surprises and Inspiration

It will be interesting this week for the class to share their discoveries of surprises and inspiration. You will also want to see how they responded to what they would look for if given three brand new days of sight.

Suggest here that some of the class members may like to keep a journal of happy memories, past and present—a journal to return to during hard times. A record book of the whole cancer experience could be a valuable resource in self-understanding. Journals can help us clarify feelings and thoughts. Many times in these classes, we will consider not what literally happened, but what you make out of what happens, what it seems like to you. These are moments when you find your depth. Participants can use their cancer experiences to define and add insight and meaning to their life pilgrimage.

Poem/Object Imagery

Fay Austin's poem (p. 37) reminds us how many thoughts, feelings and memories can be contained in one simple object. The world and objects in it are ablaze with a multitude of memories and vivid images for each of us. The exercise on p. 37 can prove to be a fruitful experience that you might wish to do again and again with objects other than the sea shell and the artichoke. I have tried it with an odd-shaped vase, but this wasn't as provocative as an item that had once been living. I also tried the experience with a uniquely-shaped piece of driftwood. Nature is bursting with objects that can speak to us in many ways and may have deep spiritual messages for us. Try this experience with something exotic, like a peacock feather. The shed skin of a snake might stir up deep, primordial images. All of these shout at us that life is more—much more—than the surface image we first see. Everything is bathed in the scintillating light of its own perfection. Objects remain the same, but we change our viewpoint. We now view the world from the perspective of the miraculous. A new point of view, a different perspective is a gift cancer brings if we allow it. Iris Murdock said, "People from a planet without flowers would think we must be mad with joy the whole time to have such things about us."

HOMEWORK FOR NEXT SESSION

Discuss the possibility of having a longer session next time for one week only. Survivors will be telling their cancer stories. Ask the class to think this week about the time they received their diagnosis, and to be prepared to share this with the group next week.

Close with Isaiah 55:12: "For you shall go out in joy and be led back in peace. The mountains and the hills before you shall break forth into song and all the trees of the field shall clap their hands."

Session 3 Guide

PREPARATION

Supplies: box of tissues; if you choose a longer time frame, you may want to have beverages for participants

WHAT WE LEARNED LAST SESSION

You are more than your cancer. It is only one part of who you are. We live in a world of beauty and surprises if we have eyes to see. We choose what to accent. After determining where we find inspiration, we can return to that source again and again.

GOALS FOR THIS SESSION

For survivors to learn about themselves by studying their individual responses to receiving a diagnosis of cancer

To look, through role-playing, at a variety of responses and try to determine each survivor's predominant attitude

To identify and admit the negative feelings cancer invokes—feelings of fear, shock, and numbness

SOME CHALLENGES YOU MAY ENCOUNTER THIS SESSION

This session is a roller coaster ride. There are definite mood changes as you move through your time together.

1. In the beginning the mood can be very intense and personal as each survivor tells his/her cancer story.
2. A breathing, imagining meditation follows each story to calm the emotions.
3. Then a third mood change occurs as the survivors look objectively at their responses and seek here some insight into their own behavior during the time of diagnosis.
4. The final mood change occurs when all of the accumulated feelings stirred up in this session find release in an art activity.

This is a session I have never been able to keep within the 1½ hour allotted time. Today is not the day to cut survivors off from telling their story in their own way and time. Neither do you want to spend the entire session just hearing each other's story without time for discussion, reflection, and interaction. If possible set a longer time for this particular session (as suggested in Session 2 Guide).

SESSION PLAN

Open this session with a prayer. Use the following, or create your own.

> Gracious God,
>
> We are coming to a difficult week on our journey and in our lives. Bless our imagination so that we may enter into each other's stories. We place our cancer stories before you, O Lord. Enlighten our lack of understanding and teach us acceptance.
>
> Amen.

Survivor Stories

Begin by allowing each survivor to have the opportunity to tell his/her story to the group. By now, hopefully, you have set a foundation for these disclosures. Trust and confidence are necessary within the group as each tells his/her story. Once you share your diagnosis with another cancer survivor there is an unspoken camaraderie that develops almost instantaneously. There is an undeniable bond.

As introduction to these stories, look in the workbook at the good and bad of telling our stories to others on p. 43. Ask the students to be alert lest they slip into repetition of their story. The danger in re-telling is becoming attached to your illness. A sign that you are becoming too attached is if you repeat the same story in the same way over and over. Then you are stuck in the story. Think of a CD that keeps going over and over in the same groove. If the group is particularly sensitive you may be able to point out when a member seems stuck.

As the stories are told feelings may overflow. Have a box of tissues on hand. This is hopefully a receptive community now, and emotions are received with empathetic understanding. We've all been there—in that scary place where terror is astonishing. All go through tough times in the beginning and again each time we are diagnosed anew. Survivors may be bearing burdens, previously undetected, of a guilty conscience or a sense of abandonment by God. It is affirming to be with persons who are willing to listen to your experience and are freely sharing their own experience with you.

After each has told his/her story, lower the lights and calm the spirits with deep, conscious breathing: then do the "bee meditation" (pp. 44-45). This creative visualization recognizes the healing potential of the mind. From emotional turmoil we move to a place of rest where our faculties are relatively calm and quiet. The challenge of visualization is remaining focused long enough for it to do its work.

Dialogue Exercises

After having heard each survivor's story, it may not be necessary to do Dialogue 1 on p. 47. However, this dialogue raises the issue of your relationship with your doctors, and someone may possibly have a comment to make on this subject. We expect so much from our doctors and become sensitive to their shortcomings and appreciative of their skills. Do not allow the group to become sidetracked here.

Move on to Dialogue 2 (p. 48). In this dialogue, the class moves from the very intense personal experience to the viewpoint of an observer. By looking at how others respond, they may gain insight into their own nature and behavior. Assign a response from the Workbook (pp. 48-49) to each member of your class. They may need a few moments to move into the mood change this activity promotes. Encourage the class to overact, to overplay these assigned responses. Emphasize that this is the response of a fictional character.

An interesting experience I had in this activity was that no one was able to do the Apology response. I'm not sure why this one was so difficult, but in two different occasions I was told, "I can't do that one—give me another one."

As the responses are being acted out, encourage other members to add comments. For example, they may have other "denial" reasons or "anger" responses. Since this is third person, a variety of options can be explored.

In doing the third Dialogue (p. 51) with the group, emphasize both the good and the bad of Acceptance and Denial. There is no correct answer here, and you want to be sure not to influence the members one way or another by showing your preference. Remember: what you judge you cannot understand. This is each person's individual answer. As they come to understand themselves, they can move confidently with the good response in either acceptance or denial.

Coloring Exercise

The art activity is entered into with a sigh of relief by the group. This has been an intense session, and a fresh package of crayons and slightly silly picture helps the members put things into perspective. This activity is usually enjoyed immensely. At first, I was hesitant to suggest such a childish activity as coloring a picture, but in all of my experiences the members loved it. It was as if they were relieved to be given permission to enjoy this simple childhood pleasure. We are dealing with a very serious adult situation with cancer, but we don't always have to be so "adult" about it.

HOMEWORK FOR NEXT SESSION

Ask the students to ponder what they have learned about themselves today. Suggest that they go back to their oak tree drawing (p. 25) and consider how they respond to cancer now, and how this may have been affected by their past. Remembering the stories of others in the class, ask them this week to pray for each other. Announce that next week the class will meet at the regular time.

Session 4 Guide

PREPARATION

Today's session dwells on treatment, and particularly three aspects of treatment: patience, endurance, and courage. Why go back there? Because as we seek to learn about ourselves through our cancer experience, we must stay with it a little longer and see what lessons it has to teach us. Your class members have suffered, or are now suffering, from a perspective that is invisible to the healthy. They are viewing their experience from the eye of the hurricane.

Supplies: Paper, pencils or pens or markers

WHAT WE LEARNED LAST SESSION

We spent the first two sessions dealing with understanding ourselves as persons loved by God, and being proud of our past and who we are now. We also affirmed what we value and stated that we ourselves are of value; each of us has some enduring and inherent worth.

GOALS FOR THIS SESSION

As we go through treatments, we tend to become a "thing." We are either a specimen to be studied or a body to be cut up and invaded. We seem to be a non-person, even a toxic waste dump. Three feelings during our time of treatment are particularly worth studying: Patience, Endurance, and Courage.

SOME CHALLENGES YOU MAY ENCOUNTER THIS SESSION

At first there may be hesitation in the group to talk about pain. We are a church group after all, and shouldn't we always be cheerful and positive and hope-filled as an example to others? We will arrive at those characteristics (cheerful, positive, and filled with hope), but only after we have gone through the hurting part and then these feelings will be more authentic because of it. Recall again Robert Frost's statement, "The best way out is always through." You must sink all the way through to discover life on the other side.

SESSION PLAN

Here is an opportunity we do not often get: an opportunity to reflect and talk about what it is like to be in pain—to witness to some of the realities of our illness.

This is an advantage in such a group as this—a group of survivors. Many times even with our caregivers, we put on a front of being brave and cheerful, and only survivors know how much energy this takes out of us. There are times when we are not cheerful and positive and hope-filled; going through treatment emphasizes this. Fear and depression are part of this experience and our suffering should be affirmed. Sometimes we want to cry, "Just leave me alone!" After all, our former life program for happiness is being dismantled. We become so obsessed with the details of our personal care that our minds become as numb as our bodies.

Chapter 4 begins by recognizing our changed status in society as a result of our illness. Social attitudes about cancer are complex. Ask the class if they have experienced these feelings of being out of the mainstream of life during their time of treatment. Going through the most severe treatment seems to weaken our link with the wider world. Persons who visit us in the hospital seem uncomfortable. And we find ourselves resenting their false cheer and hollow reassurances. "You are going to be just fine," and "Hurry back," seem like phrases of Job's comforters. Invite the class to give examples Pro and Con that they might have experienced.

Patience

Our lives are filled with waiting. Our cancer is so encompassing that we find it difficult in our live-for-the-moment culture to wait. We want it fixed, and we want it fixed *now!* While being absorbed with our inner world, two survivors found it helpful to move outside themselves by looking around them—moving from "I" to "Eye." Read Fay and Julia's responses in Chapter 4 on pp. 54-55.

It is obvious that waiting is easier for some than others. Students will try to determine their individual level of impatience. Invite them to turn to the pages in your workbook that asked for a one word description of your surroundings and share their answers. Some might want to take these adjectives and write a paragraph on what they observe. In our workbook we read: "If you are used to your needs being gratified immediately, waiting can be a lesson cancer teaches us and a reminder of how God is so patient with us." Ask, "Does this tell us something about ourselves?"

This may be the session where class members are most helpful to each other, exchanging information and survival hints. For example, you might ask for hints on being patient. What helps you wait? Some people may carry a paperback book to have available, yet to concentrate on reading requires too much effort at certain points in our cycle of treatment. Music was mentioned by one survivor. "Put on a headphone and forget where you are." Being a patient quite literally means "being patient."

Those of us raised in the Christian tradition have another wonderful resource to help us through difficult times—our faith stories. With cancer we have moved into a new landscape and we are learning to think in a different way. A faith story helps us define our new life. When we identify with a biblical story or a faith story, it gives us a slightly different focus or lens for viewing the world.

In addition to core religious stories, there are also individual stories that seem to be just for us at this time in our lives. These stories cannot be imposed on us. We must each find the story that speaks to us.

For finding your sustaining story, try this method:
- Create a list of words that describe your life at this moment.
- Look for a common theme in the words.
- Do they suggest a Bible story?

There are numerous stories and passages in Scripture that speak the truth about our current human condition and give us hope and comfort in our most difficult time. Some stories in the Bible speak of patience. We think of Moses' years in the wilderness; of Jacob's long courtship of Rebecca; of Jesus' 40 days in the wilderness; of Job, who waited in confusion and anger.

Endurance

We may find our personal story for enduring pain. One survivor found the story of Jacob's wrestling all night with an angel, to be left with a wound and a blessing, the perfect story for his cancer experience.(Genesis 32:22–31) Jane found inspiration in Jesus' story of the loaves and fishes. (Luke 9:10–17) Beth was strengthened by the story of the Vine and Branches. (John 15) Ron chose a single verse, John 10:10 "I am come that you may have life." Jody spoke of Jacob's ladder and the thought that "surely the LORD was in this place and I did not know it." (Genesis 28:16). Matthew 8:25–29, "Jesus calms the storm," was one survivor's choice. The story of Jonah spoke to another class member. If members of the class have a Bible story that speaks to them, ask them to share it.

Now consider pain. Nobody wants to hear about your pain except possibly other cancer survivors. What can we possibly learn from it?

The way to access pain is completely individual. Picking up on the spiral drawing in your workbook (p. 59), instruct your students to try some scribble drawing. All you need is paper and a pencil or felt-tip pen for each member of the class. Begin with line scribbling. Scribbling can be calming, release built-up tensions, and it is fun. More important, scribbling can help you discover your sense of self.

Consider the three states of mind in this chapter: Patience, Endurance, and Courage. Think first about Patience. Then draw a line in any direction you want on the paper, trying to capture this mood. Make the lines thick or thin, light or heavy. The lines may be straight or swirly. When you have finished, consider Endurance/Pain and follow the same directions. Finally, do a line scribble for Courage. Afterwards, think about the lines you made and the possible meaning behind them. You may discover something about yourself and how you are generally feeling about your life right now. If the group is willing, share the artwork with the others in the class. The beauty of scribble is that it transcends artistic ability—anyone can create one easily. We don't know *why* we suffer, but we can choose *how* we will experience our suffering.

Courage

We discover that there are even ways we can witness through our suffering. First, we can witness to the fact that pain and sickness are a part of every life. Just as weather contains sunny days and rainy days, so do our lives. We don't "fast forward" through this period. We hang on. This is where survivors are in their life right now. We witness through our pain that we have this moment to live and our life has value. We may pray that God will strengthen us during this period.

We are also witness to the fragility of life. We don't know why some suffer more than others. Cancer causes us to probe deeper into our faith. Some may feel that God has deserted them, but God has not left. You may want to say, "Hang in there through this painful period, and you may discover God at a deeper level of faith. Our faith is tested during great pain."

Other questions arise—Is God punishing me? Is my suffering because of something I did? Is this just a random event, or is God using me in some way or simply helping me through? Invite the participants to search their minds and listen to their hearts for answers. More important than the physiology of this disease is the impact of this experience.

Finally, we witness to the fact that we cannot answer these questions. We only learn to live with the mystery, and we affirm that we can trust God whatever our life situation.

> My grace is sufficient for you—my power is made perfect in weakness. 2 Corinthians 12:9

HOMEWORK FOR NEXT SESSION

This week, consider and ponder what you have learned about yourself so far.

Session 5 Guide

PREPARATION

Our focus for this session is on the body. With cancer we have been bombarded with high quantities of information—verbal and analytical. Our minds are in high gear, over-stimulated. What about our bodies? They respond in many dramatic ways. This session we are going to honor the right side of our brain, getting in touch with our natural instincts and imagination through accenting our senses. Put your analytical mind on hold and learn what the body itself can teach us. Trusting our intuition often guides us to do the right thing for ourselves. The changes in your physical body during cancer and the unpleasant side effects can be devastating to feelings of self-worth and acceptance.

Supplies: pages from a mandala coloring book, crayons, 8 ½ x 11 paper, sheets of art paper with a large circle drawn on it

WHAT WE LEARNED LAST SESSION

Patience, endurance, and courage are factors in cancer. Individual responses to these factors differ.

GOALS FOR THIS SESSION

- Survivors will look at a variety of ways to cope with symptoms and side effects of cancer and identify means that are helpful to them.

SOME CHALLENGES YOU MAY ENCOUNTER THIS SESSION

There are more activities suggested than you will be able to use in one session. Read through this chapter guide and choose activities that seem most appropriate to your group.

SESSION PLAN

We will think about and approach aspects of our cancer in a slightly different way than usual, using images instead of words, opening all our information-gathering channels, and we will work backwards from Chapter 5 in our workbook.

Mandalas

Begin with mandalas. Have crayons and pages of mandalas from a mandala coloring book on the table as students arrive. Invite class members to choose a mandala and begin coloring. After all have assembled, and as the coloring continues, talk informally about mandalas. Ask the participants to share what they know about mandalas from the workbook or their own experience. To stimulate discussion ask: "Are mandalas new to you? Did anyone try to create one in their workbook?" Explain that "mandala" is a Sanskrit word meaning "healing circle." Mandalas are created to bring balance, harmony, and healing into your life. Going back 2,500 years, mandalas were an art form practiced by Buddhist monks in Tibet. However this form is found in almost all cultures. The stained-glass rose windows found in cathedrals are a beautiful example of mandalas in our culture. The creation of a mandala is meant to be spiritual. Explain that we will be using them today to understand something about ourselves during our cancer experience.

SHAPE AND COLOR

We live in a world made up of shapes and colors, and we are greatly affected by them. Explain to the class that we will begin by looking at shapes, and give each student three sheets of regular 8½ x 11 writing paper.

Ask the class to think about their feelings toward their bodies at this moment. Do they feel energetic? Or lethargic? Embarrassed? Disapproving?

After determining your feelings, begin to sketch a number of different shapes on your first sheet of paper. For example: circles, squares, triangles, spheres, pyramids—as many different shapes as you can envision. Next, decide which shape best expresses your feelings toward your body. On the second sheet of paper draw your chosen shape in various sizes and locations on the paper. When you have finished, look at your pattern. Does it express your chosen emotion? Invite the class to share, if they wish, and to explain what mood or feeling each was expressing through his/her pattern. Explain that it doesn't matter whether the class agrees with you or not. These are your ideas and interpretations.

Next we want to explore what we can learn about ourselves-with-cancer through color. Each of us has certain color preferences based on our own life experiences and culture. We each make a personal response to color. For some, red may express anger. But it could also represent passion and energy. Blue may signify depression for some, but it also could express calmness.

We considered with our shape patterns our feelings toward our bodies-with-cancer. Now think about self-respect and the worth of your body.

What color represents "self respect" to you?

On your third sheet of paper, use crayons to cover the sheet with your chosen color. Experiment with the depth of the color, using other colors or the pressure of your stroke to lighten or darken it until you create the color you want. Look at your picture. Does the color reflect self-respect adequately for you?

Now students are ready to create their own mandalas.

To each participant, hand out a sheet of art paper on which you have already drawn a large circle. Give these instructions: Radiating from a center point within the circle, draw your chosen shape. Finally fill in your shape with your chosen color. Let your instincts guide you. A mandala is designed to give you space to reflect and search for self-knowledge. This mandala may express your dissatisfaction with your body-with-cancer and help you look at it in a more positive way—a way toward self-respect. Enjoy the whole process by stepping into it like a meditation.

Ask: "Did this process help bring some understanding into your views about yourself and your body-with-cancer? Or, did you find it difficult to visually represent your situation in regard to your body-with-cancer?" Invite the class members to keep their mandala and continue to study it for new insights. Their artwork contains clues to their thoughts.

Naming Side Effects

Now continuing to move backwards through Chapter 5 to pp. 72-73. Continue to consider shapes and colors here. Color and shapes enter our language to add another dimension to meaning. We use expressions like "feeling blue" or "green with envy" or "boxed in" or "circle of friends" or "love triangle." Give each of the named days either a color or a shape:

> Catatonic day
>
> Eggshell day
>
> Mule-kicking day
>
> Kryptonite day
>
> Cardboard mouth day
>
> Bad hair day
>
> Call the plumber day
>
> Rag doll weakness day
>
> Rainbow day

Share group answers.

As these mundane discomforts, created by cancer, accumulate they can take over your everyday life. Through this activity (adding a shape or color), we are attempting to shrink the proportions of our illness.

With cancer we may feel we can't trust the body to respond in its usual way. But our bodies themselves can teach us many things if we are willing to listen. Try to become aware of where you are right now in relation to your body. Ask the class members to wiggle their fingers. Tell them, "Look at your hands. The sense of touch is powerful. Often Jesus' miracles were accompanied by touch. He touched blind eyes and they opened. He stretched out a hand to a crippled woman and she stood straight." Everyone seems to know in the depth of his or her being the power of touch. We automatically put our hand to a wound, hold a sting, cradle a broken bone.

At one point during a surgical procedure I badly needed to hold someone's hand. It was a time of intense pain. Automatically I reached out and grabbed a nurse's hand. Fortunately for me, she seemed to understand my need. She stood quietly holding my hand until the procedure was completed.

Folding our hands in prayer, or bowing our heads are familiar body expressions for us as we seek to come into the presence of God.

If the group is willing to do so, experience a Bible story with your body. This is a story of healing. As a warm-up for this activity, play the Mirror game. Class members choose a partner. One makes movements with his hand and the partner mirrors those movements as completely as she can. After a few minutes of this activity, read Mark 3:1–6. Working in the same pairs, one partner represents Jesus, the healer. The other player represents the man with the withered hand. Start with the man's hand held tightly into his body. The Jesus character places his hand in a similar position. Then Jesus slowly opens his hand. The man's hand mirrors Jesus' movements. Effort and concentration are necessary. Continue until the hands freely move. Does the pantomime look like the opening of something that has been closed and lifeless for years? There is no need to explain this experience. Let the body be the teacher.

As we continue to consider our body's role in our cancer journey it sometimes helps to just stop and thank our bodies. Through great difficulties, the body works with an amazing tenacity. The life force is strong. Encourage your students to do whatever physical exercise they can during their treatment and recovery. It will help the body feel good, and that, in turn, will help them feel good.

Humor was considered in this chapter as a response to cancer. In humor we acknowledge all the negative aspects of cancer but give it a parallel view. One class was especially interested in the aspect of humor. Limericks are often a humorous form of writing and this class decided to use a limerick form to express their cancer experience. If your class would like to try this here are some rules and examples: a limerick has five lines. The 1st, 2nd and 5th line rhyme; the 3rd and 4th line rhyme.

Cancer said, "I will give you a trial.
You'll have great pain for a while"
   But the lady said, "Nope!"
   Held on to her hope
And came through it all with a smile.

Having a sense of humor is a definite advantage. Humor offers the ability to rise above a situation, if only briefly.

Your class may enjoy dealing with humor and baldness. Baldness (Alopecia) is caused not by cancer itself but by the treatments. It is a stigma, immediately identifying a cancer patient. I heard of an old Russian custom whereby students do not comb their hair the night before exams so that they do not lose concentration. We know with cancer how much concentration we lose. This is a humorous excuse to use when explaining our befuddled state: "My concentration left with my hair."

Or have the class draw some cartoons using the following captions. These captions are the basis for many cartoons, but in this instance, we apply these captions to a cancer situation. Some suggestions are given in parenthesis.

Are you sure we are on the right road? (A cancer patient in a hospital corridor being wheeled to a maternity ward)

You'll never guess what I did today. (An elderly cancer patient in a long, flowing blond wig)

What have I done now? (Nurse putting IV in the wrong place)

I don't know, I just feel lucky today. (Cancer patient being taken first in a doctor's crowded waiting room.)

Session 6 Guide

PREPARATION

Prepare pattern questions on newsprint, PowerPoint, or blackboard.
   Supplies: Apple snacks, plates, napkins

WHAT WE LEARNED LAST SESSION

There are many ways to cope with cancer symptoms. Naming them gives you a feeling of control.

GOALS FOR THIS SESSION

It is time now to end this part of our survivor's journey. It is time to pause and take stock, to consider where we have been and what we have learned.

SOME CHALLENGES YOU MAY ENCOUNTER THIS SESSION

Some participants may be unable to see patterns at this point. Explain that patterns will continue to emerge as they ponder and question.

SESSION PLAN

You were asked in the workbook, Chapter 6, to look for patterns that would help you in self-understanding. As you looked back over the past six weeks, did you notice any recurring patterns of behavior? Ask if any in the class would like to share their response.

As you continue to look for patterns, here are some questions to help you (display these questions for all to see and read):

Did any fears continue to resurface? Ponder where these fears may have come from. Is this fear from your particular cultural conditioning? Or from your own psychological make-up?

Where did you feel challenged?

Did you realize any unfinished business you need to attend to?

Did you become aware of some untapped potential in your life?

Overall do you see a pattern of optimism or pessimism?

What seemed to be your key influences during this period?

Have you found a Biblical story that is *your* story at this time of your life?

Are you dealing with the current changed circumstances of your life?

Does your cancer experience begin to fit into the larger framework of your life?

These are questions to ponder as you continue your journey. All of us have been touched in some way as a result of being challenged with cancer. Discovering patterns of behavior crystallizes new learnings about yourself. It helps clarify and reinforce new self-understandings. You may have detected some patterns you have followed, perhaps unconsciously, in building your life in spite of a life-threatening disease. What have you learned or relearned about yourself? Invite students to share answers if they wish.

You were also asked to consider the question: What has been good and what has been bad about your cancer experience? What has it given you? What has it taken away from you? Read in your workbook what other cancer survivors have said (pp. 78-79).

Many of you will have gained:

1. A strong sense of selfhood, beginning to understand and acknowledge who you are.
2. More self-confidence, making and taking responsibility for your own decisions, not immune to problems but choosing how to react to events in your life.
3. Awareness of the resilience of the human spirit.
4. The opportunity to choose the life you will now lead. Striving less to recover what you had been; more to discover what you might be.
5. A desire to be of help to others. A paradox: recognizing that we survive by helping one another and yet cancer is a journey each must make alone.
6. A deepened relationship with others, family and friends. We ask less of pity or sympathy, more of true friendship and caring.
7. A new appreciation of the gift of life itself. You have a new vantage point, which allows you to think about the value of your life, and to experience fully the importance of each day.
8. Contentment with your life as it is now after being humbled and made vulnerable by adversity.
9. Stronger spiritual tie with God. Deeper spiritual connection. One's image of God can grow broader and deeper. It is not God who is changing, but our ability to understand. Cancer can direct us toward divinity in the same unconscious way that flowers turn to face the sun.
10. Awareness of the sustaining reality of love. We do not lose touch with reality but discover a deeper realm of existence.

Ask the group, "How many of these affirmations can you affirm in your own life?"

Apples appear in our earliest biblical stories. Symbolically to taste the apple of the Tree of Knowledge in the Garden of Eden is to learn the difference between good and evil. To taste the fruits is to learn of your own mortality. In one sense, we have been offered a taste of that apple through our cancer experience.

We began these sessions visualizing ourselves as Oaks of Righteousness. Now, consider the fruits of another kind of tree, an apple tree. Imagine a bowl filled with juicy, shiny apples, deep red or golden yellow or bright green. Let this bowl of fruit symbolize your cancer experience, the good and the bad.

I love the concrete poem of Reinhard Dohl, *Pattern of Poem with an Elusive Intruder*. The poem is written in the shape of an apple. To create this shape, the word *Apfel* is repeated over and over except for one intruding word, *wurm*.

This is a good image for our bowl of apples, symbolizing our cancer experience. On each of your apples write a word stating a "good" you have received from your cancer experience (something you have gained). Now insert a worm or worm hole in your juicy apples, signifying all that you have lost with cancer. What has it taken from you?

Say, "Consider your image. Draw strength from your vision. Sketch it and share it with the group if you like."

FINAL SESSION/EVALUATION

End your sessions with apple refreshments: an apple pastry, or apple juice and cookies, or perhaps just slices of apples. Say, "May the old saying, "An apple a day keeps the doctor away" apply to your life as a survivor.

Evaluation

To help as you consider further classes you may want to have class members fill out an evaluation sheet answering such as the one below.

Design: Format as sheet of paper with lines after each question

Was the class what you expected? _____

Why did you come to the class? _____

What was *most* helpful? _____

What was *least* helpful? _____

What would you change about the class? _____